South Slavs in Michigan

Discovering the Peoples of Michigan is a series of publications examining the state's rich multicultural heritage. The series makes available an interesting, affordable, and varied collection of books that enables students and lay readers to explore Michigan's ethnic dynamics. A knowledge of the state's rapidly changing multicultural history has far-reaching implications for human relations, education, public policy, and planning. We believe that Discovering the Peoples of Michigan will enhance understanding of the unique contributions that diverse and often unrecognized communities have made to Michigan's history and culture.

South Slavs in Michigan

Daniel Cetinich

Michigan State University Press

East Lansing

⊗ The paper used in this publication meets the minimum requirements
of ANSI/NISO Z39.48-1992 (R 1997) (Permanence of Paper)

Michigan State University Press
East Lansing, Michigan 48823-5245

Printed and bound in the United States of America

09 08 07 06 05 04 03   1 2 3 4 5 6 7 8 9 10

LIBRARY OF CONGRESS CATALOGING-IN-PUBLICATION DATA
Cetinich, Daniel.
South Slavs in Michigan / Daniel Cetinich.
p. cm.—(Discovering the peoples of Michigan)
Includes bibliographical references and index.
ISBN 0-87013-643-7 (pbk. : alk. paper)
1. Slavic Americans—Michigan—History. 2. Slavic Americans—Michigan—Social condi-
tions. 3. Immigrants—Michigan—History. 4. Michigan—Ethnic relations. 5. Michigan—
Social conditions. I. Title. II. Series.
F575.S6 C48 2002
977.4'004918—dc21
2002153198

Discovering the Peoples of Michigan. The editors wish
to thank the Kellogg Foundation for their generous support.

Cover design by Ariana Grabec-Dingman
Book design by Sharp Des!gns, Inc.

COVER PHOTO: Many Croatians, Serbians, and Slovenians found
employment in the Upper Peninsula's copper and iron mines in the
nineteenth and twentieth centuries (State Archives of Michigan).

Visit Michigan State University Press on the World Wide Web at:
www.msupress.msu.edu

*This book is dedicated
to my wife Dana
and my son Aaron.*

ACKNOWLEDGMENTS

This study has been assisted by a variety of people throughout Michigan. Above all, I would like to thank my friend from our college days at the University of San Francisco, Russell M. Magnaghi, professor of history at Northern Michigan University. It was his idea that I should do this book; and after I accepted, he sent me voluminous material to aid me in my research. He made the rounds of archives and libraries for rare tidbits of information, proffered photographs from nowhere like some magician, and generally gave me succor when I was in need of help. He carefully read the manuscript, made corrections, and added interpolations. In sum, I owe him everything. I would also like to acknowledge the help of kind people at various archives and libraries of Michigan. At the Reuther Library and Archives, Elizabeth Clemens uncovered a variety of photographs for the history. In Marquette at the Baraga Association and Archives, archivist Elizabeth Delene provided information and photographs. The staffs at the Flint Public Library, Monroe Public Library and Historical Society, State Library of Michigan, Bentley Library at the University of Michigan, and Copper Country and University Archives of Michigan Technological University furnished invaluable assistance. Members of the Kordich family in Detroit (Dorothy, Carol, Donald) and in Marquette (Diane) offered important family photographs and information. Bruce Cox of Wakefield came up with an important interview concerning South Slavs in Gogebic County. In Monroe Kennie Zdelarich Kachar and Michael Kanights gave of their time to fill in aspects of that story. I must add Paulina Mijatovich, who was so kind and helpful to review this manuscript. My thanks also go to the editors of Michigan State University Press, Elizabeth Demers and Kristine Blakeslee. Finally, I would like to extend a special thanks to Arthur Helweg, professor of anthropology at Western Michigan University, for his help not only in this work but also in *American Immigrant Cultures: Builders of a Nation.*

SERIES ACKNOWLEDGMENTS

Discovering the Peoples of Michigan is a series of publications that resulted from the cooperation and effort of many individuals. The people recognized here are not a complete representation, for the list of contributors is too numerous to mention. However, credit must be given to Jeffrey Bonevich, who worked tirelessly with me on contacting people as well as researching and organizing material.

The initial idea for this project came from Mary Erwin, but I must thank Fred Bohm, director of the Michigan State University Press, for seeing the need for this project, for giving it his strong support, and for making publication possible. Also, the tireless efforts of Keith Widder and Elizabeth Demers, senior editors at Michigan State University Press, were vital in bringing DPOM to fruition.

Otto Feinstein and Germaine Strobel of the Michigan Ethnic Heritage Studies Center patiently and willingly provided names for contributors and constantly gave this project their tireless support. Yvonne Lockwood of the Michigan State University Museum has also suggested and advised contributors.

Many of the maps in the series were prepared by Gregory Anderson at the Geographical Information Center (GIS) at Western Michigan University under the directorship of David Dickason. Additional maps have been contributed by Ellen White.

Other authors and organizations provided comments on other aspects of the work. There are many people that were interviewed by the various authors who will remain anonymous. However, they have enabled the story of their group to be told. Unfortunately, their names are not available, but we are grateful for their cooperation.

Most of all, this work is a tribute to the writers who patiently gave their time to write and share their research findings. Their contributions are noted and appreciated. To them goes most of the gratitude.

ARTHUR W. HELWEG, *Series Co-editor*

Contents

Introduction

The South Slavs of Michigan—Croats, Slovenes, Serbs and Montenegrins, Bosnian Muslims, and Macedonians—are a microcosm of
the immigration saga that occurred throughout the United States.
The hard-fought struggle of the copper miners in the Upper Peninsula,
and their Christmas tragedy, and the development of the Detroit auto
industry are important contributions of the South Slavs to the growth
of not only Michigan but also the United States. A large number of
South Slavs returned to their homeland homesick, tired, or broken in
body, but those who remained sacrificed a great deal to make Michigan
what it is today. Immigration was a traumatic and alienating experience
for many who came to this country, one that scarred not only the first
generation but subsequent generations as well. This is a story that the
South Slavs need to preserve and America must acknowledge if our real
history is to be told.

The admission of great numbers of South Slavs into Michigan did
not happen without strong and bitter opposition from mainly
American establishment and business leaders, who were vehemently
opposed to labor and union demands for a just wage and safe working
conditions. They saw the involvement of foreigners in strikes as symp-
tomatic of socialist ideas from Europe contaminating the American
labor pool. They greatly feared the Bolshevik Revolution in Russia and

Homeland of the Southern Slavs.

viewed the immigrants from southern and southeastern Europe as sympathizers with the socialist and communist movements.

This campaign against foreigners originated with the Immigration Restriction League of 1894, conceived thirteen years after the great wave of immigration commenced. The league was backed by the moneyed "aristocracy" in New England and New York, but it was also supported by liberals and labor leaders, who saw American values threatened and feared the competition from cheap immigrant labor. Even though business leaders needed the gigantic labor resources provided by the new immigrants, they sought to impose literacy tests that Congress proposed to keep out unwanted southern and eastern Europeans.[1]

Contrary to the generally accepted truism, America was *not* a "melting pot." In order to protect themselves from anti-immigrant organizations, South Slavs began to join benevolent societies and labor unions in great numbers in the early part of the twentieth century, especially when prices rose during the postwar boom of 1919–20. They soon became an important component in the vast labor strikes of the boom years. These were the main obstacles confronting Michigan South Slavs as they tried to integrate themselves into American society. It is an important and untold part of American history.

South Slav Migrations in European History

The South Slavs first appear in recorded history in the sixth and seventh centuries, when they split off from the Slavic tribes that were slowly migrating into what is now Eastern Europe. According to one hypothesis, the origins of the Slavs could be linked to Iranians and Goths, but these theories of descendance are speculative, because there is little evidence beyond a few citations of Constantine Porphyrogenitus, a Byzantine emperor who wrote between A.D. 948 and 952 a treatise on geography and Byzantine diplomacy.[2]

The South Slavs slowly drifted down into the Balkan Peninsula, and probably separated themselves off into Croatian, Serbian, Slovenian, and Macedonian branches soon after their arrival. The Bosnian Muslims became a distinct group later when they converted to Islam; otherwise they are the same as the other South Slavs. Through their long history as distinct peoples, the South Slavs have forged their own traditions, which in the 1991–1995 Yugoslav wars of secession proved stronger than their sense of a shared experience.

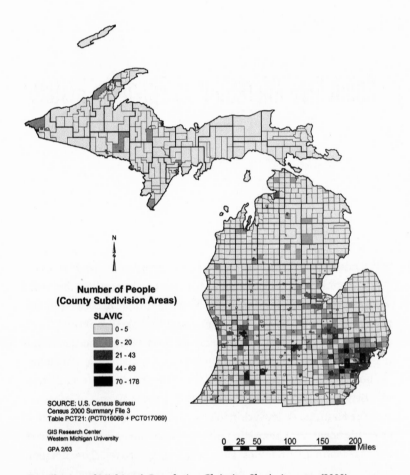

**Number of People
(County Subdivision Areas)**

SLAVIC

	0 - 5
	6 - 20
	21 - 43
	44 - 69
	70 - 178

SOURCE: U.S. Census Bureau
Census 2000 Summary File 3
Table PCT21: (PCT016069 + PCT017069)

GIS Research Center
Western Michigan University

GPA 2/03

0   25   50   100   150   200
Miles

Distribution of Michigan's Population Claiming Slavic Ancestry (2000).

Croatians

The Croats inhabit the independent Republic of Croatia, but they dwell in the other republics of the former Yugoslavia as well. Throughout their history they have had a strong affiliation with the Roman Catholic Church.

The Croats migrated from the Ukraine, and in the sixth and seventh centuries moved into present-day Croatia in the area between the Velebit Mountains and north and south of the Cetina River. Croatia was an independent kingdom in the tenth and eleventh centuries, prospering under its first king, Tomislav (914–928?), and one of its last kings, Zvonimir (1076–1089). Yet in 1102, after the lack of an heir sparked a civil war, the Croatian nobility had to unite with the Hungarian kingdom, as no Croatian leader was strong enough to control the country. A rich culture flourished from the thirteenth to the sixteenth centuries in the republic of Dubrovnik and along the rest of the Dalmatian coast, as represented by the stone sculptures of Radovan and the sculptural and architectural works of George the Dalmatian.

The crown of Croatia was transferred to the Habsburgs in 1527, and this arrangement lasted until the dissolution of the Austro-Hungarian Empire at the end of World War I. The Kingdom of the Serbs, Croats, and Slovenes was proclaimed in 1918, becoming the Kingdom of

Yugoslavia in 1929. In 1941 Axis forces invaded and divided the country, and Croatia became an independent state with Axis supervision. The Croatian fascists then perpetrated terrible atrocities on the Serbs and other minorities. The victory of the Communist Partisans under Josip Broz Tito (whose father was Croat and mother was Slovenian) in 1945 saw the creation of a federal Yugoslavia, with Croatia as one of its six republics. When Croatia declared its independence in 1991, Serbian and Montenegrin forces attacked, with hostilities ceasing in 1992 after United Nations intervention.

Why They Left and Where They Settled

The world the Croatians knew was the hilly farms of the Adriatic coast and the interior, from which in the 1850s and 1860s they began to emigrate after hearing about the opportunities in the Pennsylvania coal mines, the California Gold Rush, and the Copper Country of Michigan.[3] The peasants, 80 percent of which were landless and between the ages of fifteen and forty, worked for large landowners who were insensitive to their plight.

These men from the countryside longed to emigrate because the increase in population on the farms since the 1750s had left them in dire economic straits. The Viennese authorities had resisted the industrialization of the outer reaches of the Austro-Hungarian empire, further hardening their plight. Above all, the loss of vineyards to phylloxera blight wreaked havoc in Dalmatia. Along the Dalmatian coast, the highly skilled shipbuilders saw an impoverished future for themselves because their sailing ships had been replaced by steam-powered craft. The construction of railroads into the barren interior put local inhabitants out of work as long-distance haulers, and they were forced to emigrate as a result.[4] The subsistence farmers in the impoverished Dinaric Mountains along the Adriatic coast, whose forests had been cut down for the Venetian and Dubrovnik galleys, desired to escape conscription and political oppression. The economic pull to far-off America was strong, as letters from friends and relatives revealed it to be a land of freedom, high pay, and luxurious living, all of which were, of course, exaggerated.[5]

In the 1870s immigrant families from Severin, on Croatia's Kupa River, arrived to work for $1.25 a day as unskilled laborers in the dangerous Red Jacket copper mines of Calumet, Michigan, near Lake Superior. Among the families to arrive in 1881 were the Lesacs; their relatives and several hundred townspeople from Severin soon followed to work in the Copper Country as an intricate network of chain migrations developed. Louis Adamic's short story, "Manda Evanich from Croatia," is based upon their lives.[6] Another Lesac, Luka, sent for his wife, opened a thriving saloon, and began to raise a family. Mijo Lukas came in 1882 from the Croatian Primorje area, as did many others, and settled in Houghton. He was unschooled and illiterate and got a job with the Slovenian Peter Ruppe. He saved up enough money to bring over his wife and three sons. Nine more were to follow, and President Theodore Roosevelt sent a congratulatory telegram in 1902 when his wife gave birth to the last two—twins. One son, Anthony Lucas, would play a major role in the 1913–14 copper strike.[7]

By the turn of the century, ten thousand Croats were living in Calumet, the largest Croatian mining colony in the United States.[8] The newcomers soon started cooperatives, one of which was a grocery that began operation in 1906. By 1910 the population of the Copper Country was 90 percent foreign-born.[9]

In 1905 Emily G. Balch, the chronicler of the Slav immigration, visited the town of Severin and wrote that almost half the population of the village had emigrated to Calumet.[10] The loss of population was so extensive that the local governmental authorities in Zagreb, recognizing that this drain of its citizens was weakening the national life of Croatia, passed laws to prevent it. This was to no avail, however, since the Austro-Hungarian officials in Vienna and Budapest desired the emigration of discontented subjects, whose influence would have put too much pressure on the volatile imperial structure.

It is not an exaggeration to say that the Calumet and Hecla Mining Company (C & H) owned Calumet. The company could freely impose upon the employees dangerous working conditions, such as the use of the one-man drill (called the "widow-maker"); and the company mine shafts could be a mile in depth. C & H, owned by Bostonians Quincy Adams Shaw and Alexander Agassiz, required eleven-hour days and

Croatia

BIOGRAPHY

Joseph Vlasic (1904–86), a teenager when he arrived from the kingdom of the Serbs, Croats, and Slovenes, created the United States's largest pickle company. Vlasic Food, Inc., which he started in 1959, was headquartered in West Bloomfield Township, Michigan. In the 1970s a creative advertising campaign made Vlasic pickles famous throughout the United States. In 1978 the Campbell Soup Company purchased Vlasic for thirty-three million dollars.

Vlasic began his company on Detroit's east side with a creamery that he subsequently expanded to a business that sold milk products as well as pickles and other goods by wagon. During World War II there was a shortage of Polish pickles, so Vlasic bought pickles from Chicago and put his label on the jars. The business grew after the war, and he started making his own pickles, eventually buying a pickle plant in Imlay City. In the early 1960s he moved from Grosse Pointe, Michigan, to Scottsdale, Arizona, and his son Robert took over the business. Vlasic died in Scottsdale in 1986.

SOUTH SLAVS AND LABOR ORGANIZATIONS

Many of the South Slavs who settled in Michigan had been involved in workers' organizations and were aware of the significance of union organizing in Europe. The work of Ana Clemenc in the 1913–14 strike in the Copper Country was important in the American labor movement but it was not unique among South Slav workers in the United States. In 1926 in Detroit the Slovenian Workers Home Society and the South Slavonian Social Labor Federation were quite active in union organizing. In 1937, many South Slavs were involved with the initial organization and subsequent development of the United Auto Workers' union and with the General Motors strike. Michael Evanoff, of Macedonian background, became the union's first attorney in Flint, while his brother was its first recreation director.

CROATIAN RELIGIOUS CALENDAR

- *Three Kings (Sveta Tri Kralja):* On the Epiphany (January 6), friends are visited and gifts are exchanged.

- *Lent (Korizma):* The five weeks of fasting before Easter.

- *Easter (Uskrs):* The celebration of Christ's resurrection.

- *St. Anthony of Padua:* The celebration day of an important saint among the Croatians (June 13).

- *The Assumption (Velika Gospa):* This feast day is not only the celebration of Mary, the mother of Christ, but also is the day fields are blessed (August 15).

- *All Saints (Dan Svi Sveti):* November 1.

- *All Souls (Dušni Dan):* November 2 (or November 3, if November 2 falls on a Sunday).

- *St. Nicholas (Sveti Nikola):* An important saint's day in Croatia and other Slavic countries (December 6).

CROATIAN INDEPENDENCE DAY

Celebrated by older immigrants to the United States on April 10. When Croatia declared its independence in 1991, May 30 was chosen as the official independence day.

ADDRESSES

- Croatian Fraternal Union of America, 100 Delaney Drive, Pittsburgh, PA 15235; (412) 351-3909; fax (412) 823-1594.

- The National Federation of Croatian Americans, 1615 M Street, NW, Suite 220, Washington, D.C. 20036; (202) 331-2830.

- Croatian Catholic Union of USA and Canada, 1 East Old Ridge Road, P.O. Box 602, Hobart, IN 46342–0602; (219) 942-1191, fax (219) 942-8808.

six-day workweeks, paid $2.50 a day, and refused to recognize a union. Among the town's diverse ethnic groups, however, there was bitter and violent rivalry: Calumet was no "melting pot." The Cornish, Finns, and Irish, the Greeks and Turks, the Croats and Serbs, all despised each other. There was little acculturation in the town, as each group held on to its ethnic prerogatives.

The harsh working conditions and the workers' difficult lives resulted in the 1913–14 strike of more than thirteen thousand copper miners belonging to the Western Federation of Miners (American Federation of Labor). The strikers were inspired by Ana Clemenc (1888–1956), the daughter of a Croat mineworker and his wife, who led them every day in marches to the mines. C & H brought in armed strikebreakers from New York, the state militia, and sheriff's deputies. When two strikers were killed by the militia, the strike received international attention. John Mitchell, head of the United Mineworkers of America, renowned lawyer Clarence Darrow, and labor activist Mother Jones all marched alongside Ana Clemenc, later elected president of the Western Federation of Miners Auxiliary No. 15.[11]

The strike attracted international attention because of two tragedies. First, Croatians accidentally killed a deputy sheriff, and ten of them were tried and found guilty.[12] It was District Attorney Anthony Lucas, the son of the Croatian pioneer in Calumet Mijo Lukas, who came to the defense of the accused and pleaded for a reduction of the maximum penalty.[13] Then, in the Calumet Italian Hall at a Christmas party organized by Ana Clemenc for the strikers' children, a man, allegedly belonging to the C & H–sponsored Citizens' Alliance, which had fought against the strike, shouted a false alarm of "Fire," and over seventy-five people, a number of whom were Croat and Slovene children and adults, were crushed to death in the ensuing stampede.[14] After nine months, the strikers voted to return to work when they won an eight-hour day and a fifty-cent-a-day raise, but they still had to work six days a week and their union was not recognized by the mine owners.

The decline of the copper industry just before World War I caused the internal migration of Croatian miners from the Upper Peninsula to farming towns such as Paw Paw on the eastern edge of the Lower Peninsula's fruit and berry farms. They also journeyed to the large

"Annie" (Ana) Clemenc (Croatian) was the heroine of the Michigan Copper Country Strike of 1913–14 (Superior View Studio).

industrial cities of Flint and Detroit, where they found good jobs working for the American Car and Foundry Company and Ford Motor Company, which paid them a wage of $5 for an eight-hour day. Many flocked to Detroit's Russell Street neighborhood to become laborers, tradesmen, merchants, steamship agents, and saloon owners.[15]

Fledgling Organizations and Croat Enclaves

The first Croatians arrived in Detroit around 1890. G. Savich migrated from Pennsylvania because he had heard of the American Car and Foundry Company, where good-paying jobs were available. He contacted fellow countrymen and they came too, many moving from the Pittsburgh area. These pioneers in Detroit hailed from the towns of

Petrinja and Ogulina in Croatia's interior. They were single and willing to take any kind of job while they lived in shanties and congregated in the Russell Street neighborhood. After the workers came shopkeepers, craftsmen, and clerks. In 1907 they founded a branch of the Croatian Union, which they named the Star; and in 1913 they opened the Croatian Home on East Kirby Avenue. By 1916 there were fifteen thousand Croats in the city, the largest number situated in the Russell and Kirby Avenues area.

The majority of the immigrants believed that they would return to their homeland, and joining the Croatian Union was not an easy step for them because they did not have an understanding of or confidence in benevolent organizations, so the Croatian Union grew slowly. It was only when they saw the $800 or so that a widow received in benefits after a member's death that many Croats recognized the value of such an organization.[16]

In 1913 a branch of the Yugoslav Socialist Federation was founded in Detroit, and in 1914 the members began building a workers' center, which served as a venue for music, plays, and lectures and debates on economics, health, science, and philosophy, as well as lessons in English. After World War I, however, the persecution of immigrants involved with socialist organizations became widespread during the "Palmer raids," organized by Attorney General A. Mitchell Palmer, and 6,000 alleged communist immigrants were imprisoned in 1920. Some were tortured and 556 were deported, although they had not been convicted of any crimes. In Detroit twenty-six Croatian workers were arrested, of whom eight were eventually deported and one died in prison. Membership in the Yugoslav Socialist Federation declined during this period, and the organization never regained the vitality and membership it had before the "red scare." The federation's workers' center was sold during the Depression. As World War II raged in Europe, the Detroit federation chapter aided the struggle against fascism in Yugoslavia. The Central Croatian Organization set up a radio program, "The Croatian Radio Hour," which broadcast music and cultural programs in Croatian.[17]

In the early part of the twentieth century, Croatians had migrated from Pennsylvania to Manistique, Munising, Escanaba, and Hermans-

Croat Folk Dancers (Reuther Library, Wayne State University).

ville in Michigan's Upper Peninsula in order to work in the burgeoning logging camps and lumber mills. A number suffered injuries and death from logging accidents, but there was little or no recognition of what they had accomplished or even who they were. Most were unmarried and lived in unsanitary boardinghouse rooms that were so crowded that sometimes ten to fifteen workers had to share two or three rooms and sleep in shifts.

The greatest number of Croats, estimated at about 400,000, arrived in the United States between 1890 and 1914. Croatian emigration, however, followed the boom and bust cycle of American capitalism: in 1907 over 22,000 came, but only 2,800 migrated the following year during the Panic of 1907–8.[18] From 1900 to 1914, 33 to 40 percent of Croats in the United States, rich with money saved or broken by their grueling work, returned to Croatia.[19] Those immigrants who chose to remain would make an important contribution to the development of American industry.

At the beginning of the twentieth century, the Croat peasants who arrived in the mass migrations began to bring their wives and families. Coming from small villages, they were totally dependant on the Croatian language and the tightly-knit groups that spoke it. These Croat-speaking communities aided the newcomers in confronting the alienation and complexity of urban life. In these enclaves the immigrants were protected from the discrimination and violence of foreigners who had themselves recently immigrated and were very fearful of losing jobs to their newly arrived competitors. The Croat settlements also banded together for protection from American nativists who discriminated against all foreigners, especially those from eastern Europe.

Beliefs and Prejudice

In contrast to American individualism, Croatians in America, like most immigrants, banded together with people from their own villages and formed cooperative boardinghouses. These establishments in many ways resembled the *zadruga*, a living arrangement among large extended families, often numbering from eighty to ninety people, which was common in Croatia and Serbia. This reliance upon cooperation and family aided them in overcoming extremely harsh living conditions, and enabled their children to achieve an education and much higher standard of living.

The Croatian community began to set down roots and prosper. With the Immigration Restriction Act of 1921, however, each European nation received a quota of 3 percent of its nationals residing in the United States in 1910. The 1924 National Origins Act further decreased the quota to 2 percent and made the base year 1890, when the number of immigrants from northwestern Europe was higher. These acts thus restricted an influx of what the Immigration Restriction League viewed as less desirable immigrants from Europe's south, east, and southeast, in order to preserve "the mental and moral qualities which make what we call our race," according to Senator Henry Cabot Lodge.[20] The previous great migrations of Croats would not be repeated.

It was only after the 1940s that Croatians began to reject the traditional peasant beliefs dating from the eighteenth century of strong adherence to the Catholic religion, the family unit, social control, and discipline. Although they still played a role in family life, the traditional peasant beliefs could not prevent family structures from becoming more nuclear and less extended. Since the beginning of the twentieth century, family units had been growing smaller. The father had maintained his prominent position, and his wife was his possession: a woman bore sons and listened to her husband. It was the mother who watched over the daughters, a responsibility that she assumed gladly in order to give them a better life when they married. The father was distant from the children, although he did concern himself with his sons' education, if not his daughters'.

Social and Political Needs

The Croatians began to establish social links in the form of societies and newspapers in numerous towns in Michigan. Poet Matija Šojat founded the newspaper *Hrvatska* (Croatia) in Calumet in 1905, which published until 1936. In 1906 the Croats in that town established a lodge of the National Croatian Society, which convened there in 1909. Laymen and some Catholic priests created the national Croatian Catholic Union in 1921 to counteract the influence of the Left in Croatian fraternal organizations and newspapers such as the socialist *Radnička straža* (The workers sentinel). In 1925 the National Croatian Society became affiliated with the Croatian Fraternal Union (CFU), which soon became the largest Croatian organization in the United States and now numbers 100,000 members.[21]

In 1931 the Croatian Circle's All Croatian Congress took place in Detroit. It agitated against King Alexander's dictatorship in Yugoslavia because of its oppression of Croats. After the king's assassination in 1934, another convention of the Circle met in Detroit in 1936, and backed Dr. Vladko Maček, the president of the Croatian Peasant Party of Yugoslavia. In the 1937 United Auto Workers strike against General Motors, Croatian workers struck alongside their American coworkers at the Flint, Michigan, auto plant.[22] During World War II, Detroit hosted the All Slavic Congress, which represented all U.S. Slavic groups, with Croats in the majority. The Congress supported the war and the struggle of the

Soviet Union against the Axis powers. For many years after the war, the Croatians in Michigan were divided in their approval of the Communist government in Yugoslavia.

In the realm of education, Croats tended to send their children to parochial schools. There was a general suspicion of public schools by Eastern European Slavs, who saw them as a threat to Slavic culture. Furthermore, Magyarization of their culture by the Hungarians had made Croats especially defensive about threats to their culture. Success or material benefit through education did not impress them. For many Slavs before 1940, the purpose of education was to protect Slavic culture and morality. Because of the insecure manual labor they performed in mines, steel mills, and auto plants, those who came from peasant backgrounds were pessimistic about their survival amidst large-scale capitalist enterprises. They had many doubts about their advancement in America's class system, where material wealth meant more than spiritual values.[23]

Education among Croats became a central issue in 1940 when Adam Sudetic, a leading Croatian Fraternal Union member from Detroit, opposed historian Francis Preveden's plan to assess each member of the fraternal union one cent for the establishment of a Croatian educational organization that would facilitate Croatian children's opportunities for higher education. Sudetic argued that this plan would rob the children of the Croatian language and spawn an educated Croat elite that would intimidate working-class youth from enlisting in the CFU. In a referendum, Preveden's proposal was defeated by a two to one margin. A survey was also sent out and revealed the low educational attainment and mobility the four hundred thousand Croats had achieved in the United States by 1940.[24] Since the 1940s, however, the Croatians, like the Poles, have given strong backing to parochial schools and ethnic parishes.

After World War II, Croatian emigrants fled Yugoslavia because they had been on the fascist side. Along with the descendants of the early immigrants, these displaced persons moved to Detroit in droves for the better-paying industrial jobs at Chrysler Corporation. These new immigrants were young and well trained. By 1950 many Croats had moved to the northeast sections of Detroit. Most lived east of Woodward Avenue, near John R., and between Six and Seven Mile Roads; the rest of them scattered over other sections of the city. During the last half of the twentieth century, many Croatian-Americans migrated to the suburbs. In Detroit and its suburbs there are presently around twenty-five thousand Croatians, but many of the young are assimilating into American society and not joining Croatian organizations, and they have no knowledge of the Croatian language. No schools have been started to specifically foster the Croatian language; perhaps this is part of the inevitable mainstreaming of European ethnic groups. In order to retain young people in Croatian organizations, the Youth Club was started. Around two hundred Croats, Slovenes, and Serbians between the ages of fifteen and thirty participate in sporting and cultural events and exchange visits with their counterparts in Croatia, Slovenia, and Serbia.[25] The wars of the 1990s in the former Yugoslavia, however, have affected that fruitful exchange.

In 1989 Croatian-Americans in Michigan collected funds for the establishment of an independent Croatia. In 1991 they wrote letters to the Bush administration, asking him to recognize Croatia, as the German government began to pressure the European community to do the same. Alarmed by the human casualties of this war and the damage wreaked upon world cultural treasures such as the walled city of Dubrovnik, Croatian-Americans generously supported war relief, health care, and political organizations. A traveling exhibit of artwork by Croat and Bosnian children from refugee camps in Croatia toured the United States in order to make the American people aware of the war in Croatia and Bosnia and to raise money for displaced children, many of whom were orphaned by the war.[26] In 1995 the Croatian army regained the 30 percent of the territory it had lost to ethnic Serbs and the Yugoslav army. This could not have been accomplished without the financial support of Croatian-Americans from Michigan as well as from other diaspora communities throughout the world.

Religion and Culture

The main focus of the Croatian community of Michigan has been the Catholic Church. With the influx of Croatian immigrants to the Copper

Country beginning in the 1880s, church authorities sent Fr. Josip Polić from Croatia in 1901 to care for their needs. Accustomed to making do, he said Mass in the Slovenian St. Joseph's Church until the Croatians constructed St. John the Baptist Church, which was dedicated in 1903.[27] After the economic decline in the Upper Peninsula, many Croat mining families in Calumet were forced to head for Detroit to find work in the auto industry. Fr. Oskar Suster established St. Jerome's Croatian Church there in 1923. Less than ten years later the parish held the first annual Croatian Day Picnic on July 4, 1932, with a Mass at St. Jerome's and then a parade to St. Jerome Park.

The Croatian community in Detroit has always been small. In 1953, however, during the cold war, trouble sprang up between various factions of the community. The more assimilated element in St. Jerome's did not want "to listen to Balkan politics." Parishioners either joined other parishes or established Croatian Baptist and Pentecostal churches, driven away by what one old-timer described as the "continuous bellowing of Balkan leaders in our church." Such factionalism further diminished the cohesiveness of the Croatian community in Detroit.

Still, Roman Catholicism has been the key to the Croats' cultural expression in Michigan. Their adhesion to the Catholic faith has been manifested in an unquestioning belief in the church's dogma, and an interest in the ceremonies centered upon the sacraments of baptism and marriage. There is a strong devotion to the Virgin Mary, which can also be seen as a cultural expression. In sharp contrast to Italian culture, Croatians have not fostered anticlerical sentiments toward the clergy, whom they, like the Poles, view as authoritative preservers of their culture.

At the same time, the Croats have been much slower in establishing ethnic parishes than have the Poles. As with other Eastern Europeans, they have looked upon the priests as intermediaries in political and religious questions. The Irish Catholic hierarchy do not accept this intermingling of faith with politics; they have adopted the Protestant belief of separation of church and state. Every now and then conflicts have thus sprung up between Croatian clerics and the Irish hierarchy, contributing to the latter's resistance to Croatian ethnic parishes.

At Croatian religious festivities, music and folk dances are important cultural manifestations for the community. During Christmas, the rich tradition of Croatian choral music is exemplified in the *koleda*, secular songs that go back to the pagan winter solstice celebrations when the youth of the village visited each dwelling and sang songs in exchange for food and drink. The *kolo* (circle dance) is performed during folk festivals, with the dancers donning elaborate regional costumes. At the festivals or picnics, Croatian-Americans sing traditional songs, dance, and prepare barbecued lamb roasted on spits and *ćevapčići* (little rolls of minced meat with chives and onion and served in a bun). They also enjoy apple strudel, biscotti, and walnut bread.[28]

The *tamburica*, a stringed instrument similar to a mandolin, plays a key role in Croatian cultural life. The Detroit Tamburitza Orchestra is the best known in the state, and in 1984 was well received on its tour of Croatia and Vojvodina in Serbia. The Croatian Fraternal Union sponsors many youth orchestras in order to carry on Croatian culture. Croatian music is also being preserved due to the efforts of Zlatko Kerhin, who has collected Croatian folk art and culture in the immigrant archives at the University of Minnesota.

Since the 1950s the Croatian community in Detroit has prospered. Following the national trend among the middle class at this time, Croats began moving in the 1950s to the suburbs, where they constructed a new St. Jerome's Church in 1955. In the early 1980s, the community sold the Croatian Catholic Center and Home and built a cultural center next to St. Jerome's. The center consisted of a hall, meeting rooms, a cultural exhibit area, and picnic grounds. With the continued movement of Croat families to the suburbs, however, the number of St. Jerome's parishioners declined. Finally, in the mid-1990s the archdiocese of Detroit closed the parish. Today St. Lucy's Catholic Church in Troy has become the spiritual and cultural center for Croatians in Metro Detroit.

Croatians in Michigan have assimilated quickly into the American way of life, as younger generations have become more removed from their cultural heritage. Croats now get married at an older age. The traditional lavish weddings in ethnic halls where the bride's family expends a great deal of money have been superceded by American-style catered receptions that bear little resemblance to the Croatian affairs of the past. However, with the more recent interest by the young in their ethnic roots, Michigan Croats are searching for ways to remain a dynamic community and preserve their heritage.

Serbians and Montenegrins

The Serbians and Montenegrins are the South Slavic peoples who have opted to remain in Yugoslavia after Slovenia, Croatia, Macedonia, and Bosnia-Herzegovina declared their independence in 1991–92. Montenegrins are Serbs who share the same culture due to the dissolution of the Serbian Empire in the fourteenth century and Montenegro's isolation from Serbia because of its four-century struggle against Ottoman control but who claim a distinct political tradition. Both groups are ethnically similar to the other South Slavs. They use the Cyrillic alphabet, as do the Russians, Bulgarians, and Macedonians; Croatians, Slovenes, and many Bosnians use Latin characters. Otherwise, the literary language of the Serbs and Montenegrins is basically the same as that of the Croats.

Past and Present

During the Slavic migrations of the sixth and seventh centuries, the Serbs and Montenegrins settled the lands situated southeast of those claimed by the Croats. Byzantine missionaries, the most famous of whom were Saints Cyril and Methodius, converted them to Eastern Christianity in the ninth century. The first stirring of the Serbian people against the control of Byzantium was the creation of the ancient kingdom of Dioclea, which later became Zeta and encompassed present-day Montenegro.

The Nemanja dynasty was established in 1190 by Czar Stephen Nemanja (ca. 1190–96), and for more than two hundred years Serbia's wealth—based primarily upon silver, gold, lead, and copper mines—contributed to its growth and cultural flowering. Stephen's son, Sava, became archbishop of an independent Serbian Orthodox Church, and through his efforts it prospered. Churches and monasteries with exquisite frescoes were built throughout the thirteenth century. Continuing Serbia's expansion, Czar Stephen Dušan (1331–55) codified the laws, known as the *Zakonik,* in 1349 and was forging a Serbo-Byzantine bulwark against the Ottomans when he suddenly died and his empire fell to pieces.[29]

The threat from the Ottoman Turks reunited the Serbs under Prince Lazar Hrebeljanović (d. 1389), King of North Serbia, but the Ottomans defeated the Serbs and their Balkan allies at the Battle of Kosovo Polje (Blackbirds Field) in 1389, and in 1459 the kingdom was totally conquered, beginning a four-hundred-year domination by the Turks. Although part of Montenegro was subjugated in 1499, a large area of the mountainous country remained free and continued to resist.[30]

From 1804 to 1813, Karadjordje Petrović, a *hajduk* (outlaw) leader from Topola in Šumadija, began the liberation struggle that eventually culminated in 1878 with Serbia's independence. It became part of the Kingdom of the Serbs, Croats, and Slovenes in 1918. In order to end political chaos, however, King Alexander imposed a dictatorship in 1929, when the country assumed the name Yugoslavia.

The Axis powers took control of Yugoslavia in 1941, and three months later Marshal Tito's Partisans began the struggle against the Axis, Croat Ustaše, and the Royalist Četniks under Draža Mihailović that led to victory in 1945. Yugoslavia became a socialist republic, which lasted until the movements for independence in 1991, when the Yugoslav Peoples Army, under Serbia's president, Slobodan Milošević, began hostilities in Slovenia and Croatia, and in Bosnia-Herzegovina the following year. In 2000 Milošević was deposed and imprisoned, and in 2003 Yugoslavia broke up to form Serbia and Montenegro.

Causes of Migration and Settlement

The Serbs and Montenegrins started to emigrate to the United States between 1880 and 1914, when southern and eastern Europeans departed the Old World in massive numbers to fill the vast labor needs of the United States's industrial expansion.[31] The magnitude of the migration cannot ever be ascertained with any accuracy, since U.S. immigration authorities recorded the country of origin but not the ethnicity or cultural affiliation of immigrants. Thus Serbs could be Bulgarians, Dalmatians, Bosnian-Herzegovinians, Croats, Slovenes, Hungarians, or Austrians, because they were living in many localities in the Balkans. From 1880 to 1914, during the largest migration in history, known as "the great wave" because of the twenty million southern and eastern European immigrants who passed through Ellis Island, about one hundred thousand Serbs landed in the United States. They called their various communities here colonies, since many planned to return to their homeland.[32]

For Serbs, emigration patterns varied from region to region and involved many complex factors. Of the Serbs who left, approximately two-thirds came from either Croatia's military frontier region (*vojska krajina*), which had been the Habsburg line of defense against Ottoman advancement into Europe, or the Vojvodina area northeast of Belgrade. The former were descendants of the *graničari* (frontiersmen), who had been invited by the Habsburgs to defend the southeastern European border areas in the seventeenth and eighteenth centuries. However, in 1869 the military frontier had been dissolved due to the decline of the Ottoman Empire, leaving the settlers there with little choice but to relocate to areas where other work was available. Thus many Serbian pioneers in America did not actually migrate from Serbia proper.[33]

In Croatia the Serb immigrants left areas suffering from the economic depression of the late nineteenth century, when the rich northern Habsburg lands could not support the overpopulated Slavic agricultural areas of the south. Faced with periodic crop failures and unable to keep up with the large commercial enterprises tied to the Austro-Hungarian centers in Budapest and Vienna, the Serbs' small farms withered away, and money soon became difficult to obtain.

Serbia

BIOGRAPHY

Mike Vuich (1894–1973) was a prominent businessman in Monroe. He was born in Slavonia, Croatia, and migrated to Monroe in 1915, where he first worked for a paper company but quickly opened Red Star Lunch. In 1929 he established his first grocery store, the East Side Market. At the height of his career, he had eight Food King Markets in Carleton, Flat Rock, Romulus, Wayne, and Inkster. Vuich played a role in the development of St. George's Serbian Orthodox Church.

TRADITIONS

Yule Log: Early on in their history the Serbs celebrated Christmas Eve and Christmas Day in connection with the winter solstice. The ancient Slavs were cultivators, and the lengthening of the day was marked with a great deal of ceremony, since it was the renewal of nature, or Badnji dan in Serbian. In this ceremony the father heads out before sunrise to cut down a beech or ash tree that will serve as the badnjak or Yule log. At the evening meal the tree is brought in and the father greets his family, who toss grain upon him. A fire is lit with the Yule log, and when it burns brightly, the father carries a special loaf of bread and a glass of wine to the granary, where ceremonies are conducted to ensure a productive crop. This custom originated from old Gothic and Saxon pagan rites.

Easter eggs: At the vernal equinox, when Easter is celebrated, the Easter egg is

Furthermore, Austro-Hungarian inheritance laws required that farmers distribute their land to all sons equally, instead of to the eldest, resulting in ever smaller plots of land, which soon were not economically viable.[34] The Serbian peasants did not have a voice in the Habsburg government, yet they were heavily taxed while receiving a minimum of aid and little in the way of tools and fertilizers. Those who lost their lands in Croatian Slavonia or Vojvodina could find work only on huge estates for a pitiful wage.

Yet, the generally accepted myth that the poorest inhabitants of an area are the first to emigrate does not bear up to careful scrutiny in the an important symbol of the vernal rebirth of nature. The coloring of eggs goes back to the Persians, and for the Serbs the bright colors are emblems of spring blossoms.

Vidovdan (St. Vitus Day, June 28): This holiday commemorates the Serbian defeat at Kosovo Polje in 1389 at the hands of the Ottoman Turks and their subsequent domination for four hundred years.

ADDRESSES

- Serb National Federation and Amerikanski Srbobran (The American Serb Defender), 1 Fifth Avenue, Pittsburgh, PA 15222; (412) 642-7372 or (800) 538-SERB; fax (412) 642-1372; snf@serbnatlfed.org; http://www.serbnatlfed.org/.
- Serb World USA, 415 East Mabel Street, Tucson, AZ 85705-7456; (520) 624-4887.
- St. Lazarus Serbian Orthodox Cathedral Ravanica, 4575 East Outer Drive, Detroit, MI 48334; (313) 893-6025.
- Serbian Singing Society Ravanica, 19940 Van Dyke Street, Detroit, MI 48234; (313) 885-4091.
- Holy Ascension Serbian Orthodox Church, 4337 West Jefferson Street, Ecorse, MI 48229; (313) 388-9721.
- American Montenegrin Cultural Club Lovčen and Montenegrin Education Club, 28125 Grand River Street, Farmington, MI 48024; (313) 979-7899.

Serbs' case. Serb peasants living in the hinterland of Serbia had much less opportunity or inclination to emigrate because they had regular employment on well-off family farms, had not heard about the wealth of America from early immigrants, or simply could not afford to emigrate.[35] Resourceful Serbs, however, inhabiting districts in Croatia's military frontier like Lika-Krbava, had more incentive to emigrate, because of their economic ability to transplant themselves and also due to the Austro-Hungarian policy that limited industry in parts of the empire that would compete with Austria or Hungary proper. Since these individuals were frustrated in utilizing their entrepreneurial skills and what they had picked up as apprentices, they therefore were more likely to emigrate.

Ethnic and religious persecution also played a part in Serb emigration. Under Ottoman expansionism, the Habsburg Empire had made compacts that protected the culture and religion of the Serb peasant soldiers. When the Ottomans were no longer a threat, these guarantees were ignored and the *graničari* were subjected by the Hungarian rulers to a Magyarization campaign in the agriculturally rich Vojvodina district. Schools and courts were required to use the Hungarian language instead of Serbian, and Serbs were pressured to convert to Roman Catholicism not only by the Hungarian government but also by their fellow Croatians, who called the Serbs Croatian Orthodox.[36]

Many Serbs and Montenegrins (the latter emigrated during the rule of King Nikola Petrović-Njegoš, 1860–1918) fled the area to avoid military conscription, especially during the Balkan Wars of 1912–13, when they falsified passports and other documents to hide their nationality.[37] Serbs also emigrated to escape oppressive and impoverished areas of the Austro-Hungarian Empire. In regions of harsh poverty, such as Lika or Srem in Croatia, or in Herzegovina, the peasants heard about the great wealth of America from well-off friends and neighbors who had returned. It is believed that most of those early immigrants had no intention of remaining in the United States, preferring to return after amassing a certain amount of wealth.

Many of the Serbs who left, since they were not on the lowest rung of society, were literate and possessed certain skills that would help them in learning the requirements necessary in their new industrial jobs in the United States. American employers would greatly benefit from these immigrant employees, who brought with them work habits acquired as apprentices in the European labor markets.[38]

In the 1880s Serbs from Croatian Slavonia, Vojvodina, and Bosnia-Herzegovina, or areas of the Ottoman Empire, as well as Montenegrins, headed for the industrial centers of the Midwest and East, and the mines of the West. This was all part of an internal chain migration, beginning in the coal mines of Pennsylvania, moving on to the copper mines of Michigan, and then finally on to Detroit or Flint, where the immigrants found work in the factories.

Serbian wedding of Frank and Nellie (Sokolov) Elderlon at the St. Lazarus Serbian Orthodox Church, Detroit, ca. 1927 (Kordich Family).

Serbian Communities in Michigan

Serbian immigrants began to arrive on the Gogebic Iron Range in the 1890s. Most found jobs in the iron mines that dotted the country between Wakefield and Ironwood. The entrepreneurs among them operated small businesses when opportunities arose. Since their numbers were small, the Serb settlers had to travel to Duluth to attend Christmas or Easter liturgies at St. George Serbian Orthodox Church. Serbs were not the only South Slavs to settle Gogebic County, as they were joined by Croats and Montenegrins. In 1939 the American All Slav Club of Gogebic County was incorporated at Ramsay. It united "all Slavic races" of the county and provided them with a place to meet and exchange ideas for mutual benefit.

Most of the Serbs arriving in Detroit came from Vojvodina and were peasants who had little or no education. By 1908 Detroit's East Side included about three thousand Serbs, who congregated in three neighborhoods: Russell Street, Clairpointe Avenue, and the Six Mile/Davison/Oakland area.[39] There were numerous boardinghouses, and each community had its own hall for social gatherings. The typical boardinghouse had neither water nor electricity, nor other amenities for that matter. The courtyard contained a water pump and stalls for washstands. The houses were usually of two stories, with three rooms on each floor. On the ground floor would be the landlord's room, the dining room, and the kitchen; on the second floor were three bedrooms where up to eighteen immigrants slept. Each room featured three iron beds in which two men slept at a time.[40]

Many Serbian meat markets and grocery stores were opened in the Russell Street neighborhood. The Russell Theater drew people from the community, and Serbian could be heard there. It was like a small-town neighborhood, where people knew each other. During World War II, Detroit was even visited by King Peter II, and Vasa Milich, a worker in the Chrysler Tank Factory, converted to war production, gave him a tour through the plant.[41]

Serbs from the Balkans and other locations in the United States began to migrate to Ecorse and Monroe around 1912. They found jobs at Great Lakes Steel in Ecorse. Women established boardinghouses within the shadow of the mill. Other Serbs were employed at the numerous paper mills around Monroe and at Monroe Auto Equipment Company and Detroit Stoker Company. Between Monroe and Pontiac, some Serbs obtained employment with the numerous railroads that operated there. Small businessmen like grocer-butcher Ted Zdelarich and grocer Mike Vuich started shops in their neighborhood, which was located at the east end of Monroe. Vuich eventually expanded his chain of groceries as far north as Romulus. Serbian Hall was built in the 1920s and served as a cultural and social center for the small Serbian community. It also doubled as a chapel when priests came down from Detroit for services. In 1960 St. George Serbian Orthodox church was completed and dedicated. Two picnic grounds were used by the Serbians, who roasted the traditional lambs and pigs at social gatherings.

Some Serbs heard of the opportunities in Michigan's Upper Peninsula and found jobs in the copper and iron mines and in the lumber industry. The story of Ilija Miljevich is typical of not only Serb immigrants but many immigrants who became successful in the United States. It is a complex story involving changes of occupation and chain migration, but immigration to America is itself a complex saga of the largest mass movement of people in history.

In 1908 Ilija Miljevich came to America from Bosnia. He first went to Alaska, then moved on to Washington and Oregon. When he heard that many Serbs were living in Minnesota's Iron Range, where they had their own churches and possessed halls for social purposes, he decided to join them. He went into the saloon business with a partner and decided that the time was right to send for his family. When his partner absconded with the bank account, Ilija moved his growing family to Michigan's Upper Peninsula. In 1914 he settled in Wakefield, Michigan, and became a miner. He rented a large house, where he and his wife provided room and board to forty miners. During the winter, the pit closed down, and the Miljeviches relied on credit to get through until the spring and the mine's reopening. Ilija bought a farm in Wakefield when mining declined, and he constructed a house, a barn, chicken and pig sheds, and a smokehouse. In 1929 Ilija purchased seventy acres of virgin timber south of Wakefield in Chaney Lake, where the family eventually built a sawmill and started a small logging and lumbering operation, which gradually expanded.[42] Serb families like the Miljeviches were not unusual, and played a key role in the development of vast tracts of Michigan's forests and farms.

Other Serb immigrants found jobs in the auto industry due to their specialized training. Isa (John) Sandich arrived from Serbia with experience as a wagon and furniture maker. Because of his excellent woodworking skills, he was hired by General Motors as a maintenance carpenter. When needed he was employed by the Fisher brothers to work on their country home. In his free time he helped friends construct their own homes, and he augmented his GM wages by building a new home on inexpensive land on the outskirts of Detroit. The home was completed, lived in for a time, and a new one started while the previous home was sold for a profit.

Serbian and Montenegrin migration slowed to a trickle because of the Balkan Wars of 1912–13 and World War I, when thousands of Serbs in the United States returned home to fight for Serbia. After the war, the Immigration Restrictions Act of 1921 gave each European nation a quota that was based on 3 percent of the number of its citizens in the United

States in 1910. This act would limit immigration to around 350,000 persons anually, mostly from northwestern Europe.

The National Origins Act of 1924 further restricted quotas to 2 percent and used the base year of 1890, when the proportion of immigrants from southern and southeastern Europe had been much smaller and the number from northwestern Europe much greater than in 1910. The 1924 act would be in force until 1927, when only 150,000 immigrants were to be admitted anually, based on the ratio of each country's citizens to the American population of 1920. During the Depression from 1931 to 1939, immigration varied from 12,000 to 63,000 Europeans each year. The immigration laws of 1921 and 1924, which discriminated against South Slav immigrants, drastically reduced their immigration.

The Serbs who sought asylum from Yugoslavia after World War II congregated in areas where earlier immigrants were living. With the defeat of the Četniks, thousands of these displaced persons (politicians, lawyers, and army officers among them) were welcomed in the United States. Having supported King Peter II during the war, they migrated not to flee poverty, as their predecessors had, but because of their anti-communist views and their opposition to Marshal Tito. The Serbian Orthodox Diocese and *Srpska Bratska Pomoč* (Serbian Fraternal Aid) settled 350 of these displaced persons after World War II, many of them finding jobs with Chrysler Corporation. Since most of the refugees came from Bosnia-Herzegovina, half of the congregation of St. Lazarus Cathedral Ravanica were Bosnian Serb émigrés. By the end of the 1940s, much antagonism had erupted among the émigré groups, and despite efforts by the Serbian National Defense's president, Mitchell Duchich, to get them to cooperate, the groups did not come together. They were urban and well educated, and therefore were able to create new organizations and newspapers, revitalizing the contending factions.

Fifteen hundred individuals and family members arrived in Detroit via Italy, Austria, West Germany, and France in the early 1950s. They were sponsored in the main by families of the St. Lazarus Serbian Orthodox Ravanica parish, aided by loopholes in the 1953 Refugee Relief Act, since the existing immigration laws would not have allowed their sponsorship. The greatest number came from the Tetovo area of Macedonia, while a quarter originated in the Vojvodina district of Serbia.[43]

When the Yugoslav borders were opened in 1965, more Serbians were drawn to Detroit in order to pursue better opportunities in the United States. There were many professionals among them, having received a good education in the new Yugoslavia. They were very different from the earlier immigrants, who had arrived after the turn of the century, in that they lacked interest in church-related functions. Yet the Orthodox Church served as a link to their culture, and still figured in the social life of many.

Dragan Vraneš, a direct and practical man, is a Krajina Serb who left Yugoslavia in the early 1970s and now has a business in Hamtramck that does construction and decorating; he also rents out six houses that he owns.[44] Unlike Vraneš, the latest immigrants, especially those who have fled the recently ousted Milosević regime, have come to the United States to advance their careers: many are engineers or in other professions and seek training here.

Many Serb immigrant women found that their work was dominated by home life in the early years. Their lack of understanding of the English language made outside employment impossible. Some, like Saveta Sandich, brought skills with them that aided their plight. Saveta was a seamstress in the Old Country, and although she did not go into business in Detroit, she did sew clothes for her family, which greatly aided their finances. Other women took in boarders and augmented the weekly rents with profits from the sale of homemade wine and whiskey. Second-generation women were in a better position to find employment outside the home. Mary Kordich, who lost her husband in the 1930s, was provided a job by her husband's former employer. For many years she worked on the assembly line at the Dodge Main plant in order to raise her family of four children.

Church-related organizations among Serbian women were and continue to be active. Since its founding in 1931, the Serbian Singing Society has had many women in its ranks. St. Lazarus Ravanica's Sisters of Ravanica raise funds through dinners and bake sales for church expenses, while the Ravanica Mothers Club oversees the children in Sunday school. When these groups or the many church-related basketball or golf teams go on out-of-town trips, men and women profit from the opportunity by renewing old acquaintances.

Religion

Father Dušan Trbuhovich came to Detroit to prepare for the establishment of the first Serbian parish, St. Lazarus Ravanica, in 1917. Cveta Popovich, who had worked with the Mexican artist Diego Rivera, painted the murals for the new church, which was consecrated in 1934. Father Miodrag Mijatovich arrived in Detroit in 1943, during the height of the war in Yugoslavia. He oversaw the completion of a new St. Lazarus on East Outer Drive in 1967, and was the mainstay of the Serbian community until his death in 1976.[45]

Over the years other Serbian Orthodox congregations developed as the population increased. St. Petka's opened in Detroit and St. Stevan Dečenski was established in neighboring Warren. In the downriver community of Ecorse, Holy Ascension Church was founded, while to the south in Monroe St. George's Church was dedicated in 1960.

Contrary to the accepted myths, religion among the Serbs has been rife with rancor and division, as is true for many immigrant groups. In the last thirty years the expanding Serbian Church in Michigan has been beset with division and vituperative controversy about two related issues. In 1963 the Holy Synod in Belgrade relieved Bishop Dionisije, head of the U.S. Serbian Church, of his duties after he was accused of misconduct by American and Canadian Serbs. He refused to accept the tripartite division of the diocese, each with its own bishop, who as a result of the breakup would not have been under his jurisdiction. Under the influence of Dionisije, a diocesan assembly, controlled by World War II refugees, royalist émigrés, and anti-communist American Serbs, met twice to arrange a secession from the Holy Synod in Belgrade, claiming that it was under communist domination. This split the American church into two factions whose differences lay in their acceptance or rejection of Belgrade's authority. Thirty percent of the church's members supported independence, whereas 70 percent chose to remain loyal to the patriarch in Belgrade. Bitter public recriminations that at times divided families resulted in court cases over churches and property, and occasionally violent altercations that required the involvement of the police. The schism created havoc as churches were abandoned or fought over and new churches were built.

Christmas celebration at St. Lazarus Serbian Orthodox Church, Detroit, in 1954 (Reuther Library, Wayne State University).

In 1976 the U.S. Supreme Court decided in favor of the Belgrade faction, but this did not end the dispute. Only the dismemberment of Yugoslavia reconciled the warring groups, which were reintegrated in 1998.

Organizations and Culture

The Serb National Federation (SNF), which was founded in 1901 to foster athletic and cultural events, has been the preeminent Serb organization in the United States. It publishes the *Amerikanski Srbobran* (American Serb Defender), the most important Serb newspaper, out of Pittsburgh. The SNF's two lodges in Detroit are the Kosovo and Beograd. Two women's groups are the Udružene Srpkinje (Association of Serbian Women) and the Serbian Sisters Ravanica. The post–World War II upsurge in Serbian immigration witnessed an expansion of activities in Detroit, and in 1953 the American Serbian Memorial Hall was built. Like the Croats, the Serbs promote sports within their community. Youth basketball teams are organized around Orthodox churches and play other Orthodox teams in the Midwest. Popular golf outings also unite community members throughout the United States.

The heart of Serbian cultural life can be found in its attachment to Orthodox traditions. It is by means of the *krsna slava* (family patron saint's day) that Serbs commemorate the family's conversion from paganism to Christianity. Each element in the ritual symbolizes connection with the hearth, the departed members of the family, and the patron saint. The most important feasts are Easter, with its intricate coloring of eggs and lamb dinner, and Christmas, with its Yule log and the honey cake with a lucky coin hidden within. Liturgical music also plays a central part in these religious holidays. The Serbian church choirs of Michigan are members of the national Serbian Singing Federation (SSF), patterned after Detroit's Serbian Singing Society Ravanica.[46] The SSF was founded in 1931, and was directed for many years by Vladimir Lugonja. These cultural and religious expressions reveal the richness and energy of Serbian communities in Michigan, an important contribution to the ethnic diversity of the state.

Slovenians

The Slovenians live in the northwestern corner of the former Yugoslavia. In 1991 the 1,700,000 Slovenes voted to become an independent republic. They are not distinct from the other South Slav groups ethnically, but they speak a Slavic language that is different from Croatian and Serbian, although there are numerous words in common. They are predominantly Catholic, as are the Croatians.

The Slovenes had been under Habsburg rule since the fifteenth century, and with Austria-Hungary's collapse in 1918 became part of an independent Yugoslav nation. During World War II, Slovenia was divided up among the Axis powers, but with the Partisan victory in 1945 and the reconstitution of Yugoslavia, it became the Republic of Slovenia, with the constituent republics of Croatia, Serbia, Bosnia-Herzegovina, Macedonia, and Montenegro. Slovenia seceded from Yugoslavia in 1991.

Settling Michigan's Frontier

It was through the efforts of the ascetic and self-sacrificing Slovenian priest Bishop Frederic Baraga (1797–1868) that Michigan began to attract Slovene settlement. He was instrumental in the development of

Michigan's Upper Peninsula and the Midwest, doing missionary work among the Ottawa and later Chippewa Native Americans. In 1831 he established his first mission in the wilderness at Arbre Croche on Little Traverse Bay. He worked at the mission he founded in L'Anse (1843–53) in present-day Baraga County, where he later purchased the land and deeded it to the Chippewa in order to prevent their removal to the West. He also sought to instruct the Chippewa and Ottawa in trades, such as carpentry. He was an expert on the difficult Ottawa and Chippewa languages, and compiled a dictionary and grammar of the latter. In 1853 he was appointed bishop of northern Michigan and chose Sault Sainte Marie as his diocesan seat, constructing his own house, which still stands today. Because of its growing importance, the Upper Peninsula town of Marquette became the seat of the diocese in 1866. Bishop Baraga died there two years later.

With the coming of Bishop Baraga to Michigan, numerous Slovenian priests followed his example and served both the Native American and white populations. One of these priests was Father Francis Pirc (1780–1880), who was born in Godić, Slovenia. Influenced by Bishop Baraga, at age fifty he decided to work as a missionary in North America. He ministered to the Native Americans and was a fervent champion of their political and personal rights, utilizing his horticultural skills in his teaching. He served in Michigan, on the north shore of Lake Michigan, and in Minnesota.

The Lure of Michigan and the Early Pioneers

In the nineteenth century the Austrian provinces of today's Slovenia possessed very little industry and were made up mostly of small family farms. The younger sons in the families, who could not inherit land since that was the right of the eldest through primogeniture, were forced to seek their fortunes elsewhere. The reasons why the Slovenes emigrated from their homeland were as diverse as the immigrants themselves, but it is safe to say that usually it was the disadvantaged who left, but not the poorest, since they did not have the economic wherewithal to uproot their existence.

Between 1850 and just after World War I, the majority of Slovenian

Frederic Baraga (1797–1868), born in Slovenia was a missionary to Michigan's Native Americans and first bishop of the Catholic Diocese of Marquette. (Bishop Baraga Association and Archives).

immigrants to the United States came from the poorer region of southeastern Slovenia, which borders on Croatia. Provinces such as Carniola and Styria contributed a large number of immigrants, forming the first wave; and it was these unskilled laborers who spread the word about the opportunities in America to their fellow Slavs in Croatia. It is difficult to determine the number of Slovenian immigrants accurately because of the intermingling in the records of groups in the Balkans on the part of U.S. immigration officials, but it is estimated that between 400,000 and 500,000 Slovenes emigrated to the United States,[47] although a more conservative number might be 250,000 to 350,000.[48]

Slovenia

BIOGRAPHY

Philip Ruppe (1926–), a descendant of Peter Ruppe, one of the original Slovenian pioneers, was a Michigan representative to Congress from 1967 to 1979. He was born in 1926 in Laurium, Houghton County. In 1944 he went into the Navy V-12 program. He earned a B.A. from Yale University in 1948 and served in the U.S. Navy during the Korean War as a lieutenant. He was a president of a brewing company, and a bank director in L'Anse, Michigan. In 1968 he was elected to Congress, and he made an unsuccessful bid for the Senate in 1982. He was president of Woodlak Company until 1986. His wife, Loret, died of ovarian cancer in 1996, and Mr. Ruppe now resides in Bethesda, Maryland.

BIOGRAPHY

Anton Ivan Rezek (1867–1946) was a Slovenian priest and scholar born in Radovica, Slovenia. He was educated in Ontario, Canada, before emigrating to the United States and being ordained in 1890. After a few minor assignments, between 1895 and 1946 Father Rezek was pastor of St. Ignatius Church in Houghton, Michigan. Father Rezek was also a historian. In 1907 he published his monumental two-volume *History of the Diocese of Sault Ste. Marie and Marquette*, which

Before the great waves of immigration at the end of the nineteenth century, most Slovene men arrived alone or with a few other countrymen, later sending for their wives, children, and relatives. Then neighbors from the same town or nearby villages arrived, thus establishing a pattern of settlement of people from the same area in one town or region of the United States, a pattern common for most nationalities.

The cry for laborers in Michigan came from the copper mine owners in the Upper Peninsula after the Native Americans, in the Treaty of La Pointe (1842), gave up their rights to the land following the copper survey report of Douglass Houghton.[49] In 1856, at the urging of Bishop Baraga, Joseph Vertin (the father of Bishop Vertin) and Peter Ruppe, who were itinerent peddlers of watches, clothing, and kitchen utensils, headed for Michigan's Copper Country.[50] Slovenes began to settle in was praised for its scholarship at the time and still remains an important work in Michigan history.

SLOVENIAN SPECIALTIES

Potica is a pastry filled with walnuts and raisins, honey, or tarragon, while *strudel* contains a filling of apples, cherries, apricots, or cheese. *Krofi* is similar to the doughnut, and *flancati* is a flaky, deep-fried pastry. Dumplings are filled with meat or liver and cooked in soups. Carniolan sausages (*kranjske klobase*) are a specialty from the province of Carniola.

ADDRESSES

- Amerikanski Slovenec (American Slovenian), 708 East 159 Street, Cleveland, OH 44110; (216) 541-7243.
- Prosveta (Enlightenment), 247 West Allegheny Road, Imperial, PA 15126; (412) 695-1100.
- Slovene American Club, 18616 Allen Road, Melvindale, MI 48122; (313) 381-3434.
- Slovene National Home, 17133 John Road, Detroit, MI 48203; (313) 867-9504.

Hancock in 1858, and later in Calumet, after the arrival of Ruppe and Vertin. Peter Ruppe, Calumet's first mayor, opened a department store that afterward had to compete with the bigger Vertin Brothers store, which became the largest department store north of Milwaukee.[51] By 1866, when the Tamarack mine was opened in the vicinity of Calumet, Slovenians had begun to emigrate in ever increasing numbers. Most worked in the mines, while others labored at unskilled jobs and saved their money to go into business ventures.[52]

In the early 1880s an ever larger number of Slovenes poured into the copper and iron mines or the lumber camps in the Upper Peninsula and the iron country of Minnesota. They traveled from one town to another, looking for employment, mostly doing unskilled mine labor in towns like Calumet. The Slovenian population in Calumet reached five to six thousand before the end of the nineteenth century, and there were settlements in Manistique and Iron Mountain as well.[53] By 1895 half of the Slovenian immigrants to the United States had returned to their homeland, and those who remained spread across the Midwest and West, working long hours at low-paying and dangerous jobs.

Because of a labor shortage, lumber company agents searched throughout the United States for lumbermen. They found Slovenians, who were much sought after because of their woodworking skills, in Pennsylvania, and hired sixty-five young men, who arrived in northern Michigan's Alger County in 1906 to begin cutting the hardwoods. Typical of these young men was Anton Knaus, who settled in Traunik, Michigan (named after a town in Slovenia), in 1910. Though they first came to Michigan on their own, these Slovenes soon brought their wives and daughters to join them. The wives cooked and baked for the lumberjacks, their days beginning at 4 A.M. and ending at 9 P.M. Emma Knaus remembered being paid ten dollars a month for the work she did.[54]

Ivan Molek (1882–1962), author, journalist, lecturer, and publisher, was born near Metlika, Slovenia, and arrived in Calumet on a snowy day in May 1903. He was able to find a job in the Calumet copper mines. He later became the editor of *Glasnik* (The Herald), Calumet's Slovenian paper. In his autobiography he wrote, "and thus did the former herdsman and thresher, the former vine-grower, the former steel 'laborer' and the former miner leap directly from the mine to the editor's desk. . . . I would never have made this bold jump in the old country. This was possible only in America—the wonderful land of all possible opportunities." He soon attacked the Slovenian clergy for taking money from workers. He especially singled out Father Luka Klopchich, which resulted in his being blacklisted in Calumet and having to leave for Chicago, where he became editor of *Proletarec* (The Proletarian) in 1907.[55] From 1916 to 1944 he was the editor of *Prosveta* (Enlightenment), the leading Slovenian newspaper in the United States.

In the 1910 U.S. census a small number of Slovenes were listed as working in the lumber industry in the Marquette County townships of Ely, Ishpeming (205 Slovenes worked at the mill), Marquette, Powell, and Tilden. In the village of Big Bay (Powell Township), there was a boardinghouse referred to as the "Austrian Hotel." Slovenians probably rented there, since they called themselves "Austrian" when they arrived in the United States, as the Slovenian provinces were part of Austria-Hungary at that time.[56]

After the copper strike of 1913–14 in the Upper Peninsula, many Slovenes moved to other states or started farming. As the forests were cut down, farms replaced the lumber camps and the Slovenian community settled down to a new life. Traunik had a post office by 1927, and the town expanded. Farm chores such as haymaking, hog butchering, and tending to the chickens were women's tasks, as was caring for the house and children. After World War II, Traunik went into decline as the second generation moved to large cities to find higher-paying jobs in the industries of the Lower Peninsula.

The first known Slovenian in Detroit was Joseph Faletich, who opened a saloon in 1903.[57] Saloons were profitable businesses for those immigrants who learned English quickly, and they served as a center for the social and business activities of newcomers. Saloonkeepers acted as ticket agents for companies that brought over immigrants, as well as being bankers and intermediaries between the immigrants and local authorities. Although immigrants might lose a great deal of money at the saloons, they were also places where they could meet their fellow countrymen on Saturday or Sunday nights and holidays. There they could listen to *tamburica* bands, hear Slovene, Croatian, or Serb songs from the old country, and enjoy the warmth of familiar fellowship in an otherwise alien environment.[58] They went to the saloons not only to drink but also to receive advice and political news about Slovenia from bar owners, who often were members of the various political organizations and mutual aid societies.

After World War I, when most of the Calumet and Hecla Company mines cut back production because of the lack of demand for copper, Slovenians migrated to Detroit to work at the steel foundries, and in the automobile and related industries, where there was a demand for skilled workers. Others moved to Flint and Saginaw, while many sought industrial employment in the other cities of the Lower Peninsula. Of the eight thousand Slovenes in Michigan today, most are concentrated in Dearborn, Detroit, and suburbs like Troy.[59] The Slovenes have very quickly managed to integrate themselves into the

American mainstream. Philip Ruppe, a descendant of the pioneering Ruppe family of Calumet, served in Congress from 1967 to 1979 as a Republican representative.

Fraternal Societies and Newspapers

Since it was the mining industry that first attracted Slovenes to the United States, it was around that livelihood that the immigrants began to organize, as the mine owners made little or no provision for the workers' safety, or for injury or death compensation. Before the 1880s, the Slovene mine workers belonged to a German fraternal society. Because of the great influx of Slovenian laborers in the early 1880s, however, they set up the first Slovenian Fraternal Benefit Society in Calumet—St. Joseph's Lodge—in 1882. Sick benefits were fifty cents a day, and at the death of a member the others each paid a dollar for death benefits.[60]

The first Slovenian fraternal insurance society was the Carniolan Slovenian Catholic Union, which was founded in 1894. In 1966 it became known as the Slovenian Catholic Union, and this organization currently has more than forty-five thousand members. In 1904 the Slovene National Benefit Society (SNBS) was formed, and by 1921 it had become the immigrants' social and cultural focus, since there was a general reluctance to use the Slovene churches as means of cultural expression, due to a mistrust of the clergy. The SNBS currently has seventy thousand members in the United States, with fourteen lodges in Michigan.

The SNBS's newspaper, *Prosveta* (Enlightenment), is still published in Pennsylvania. *Ameriska domovina* (American home) and *Amerikanski Slovenec* (The American Slovenian), both out of Cleveland, along with *Prosveta*, are the most important Slovene newspapers printed in the United States. Although no longer published, the socialist paper *Proletarec* believed that Slovene workers had to have a professional education to help them find jobs and serve as a bulwark against exploitative bosses. In its pages it argued that Slovene children needed schools that fostered science for their economic betterment. *Proletarec* promoted the Yugoslav Educational Association, which provided free lectures and information on "The Value of Education" and "Birth

A Slovenian in 1931. These South Slavs were first attracted to the Upper Peninsula by Bishop Baraga. Many moved to Metro Detroit during the metro boom of the 1920s (Reuther Library, Wayne State University).

Control."[61] It is interesting to note that socialists represented a higher percentage among Slovenes than among Croats, because there had been more industrialization and concomitant socialist ideas in the Slovene homeland, ideas that thus spread to a number of immigrants bound for the United States. By 1905 in Calumet, Michigan, the Slovenes and Croats had come together to form the Slovenian-Croatian Union. The largest Slavic socialist movement, the Yugoslav Socialist Federation, was founded in 1910 among the South Slavs. It was soon enmeshed in ethnic arguments between Serbs, Croats, and Slovenes. All three groups, however, were in agreement in their critique of the materialism and secularism of urban America and the lack of morality in the vaunted U.S. industrial miracle.[62]

Before war broke out in 1991 between Slovenia and the Yugoslav federation, Michigan's Americans for Free Slovenia, the *Ameriska domovina* (American home) newspaper, and the Slovenian Research Center of America had already begun working for the recognition of Slovenia's independence, which came in 1992.

The Church and Ethnic Identity

For almost the entire second half of the nineteenth century, all the bishops of the Catholic diocese of Marquette—Frederic Baraga, Ignatius Mrak, and John Vertin—were immigrants from the same Slovenian province of Carniola. This was probably the only such occurrence in the history of the American Catholic Church.

In the early 1880s, the Slovenians in Calumet used Sacred Heart Church for Mass, but in 1890 Bishop Vertin consecrated a new church, St. Joseph's, for the Slovenian congregation. In December 1902, St. Joseph's burned to the ground, and it was not until 1908, when Father Luka Klopchich was pastor, that a new sandstone St. Joseph's was completed. The impressive church is still standing as a monument to the faith of the Slovenian immigrants. The Slovenian church gained more faithful after the 1913–14 copper strike, when members of the Polish community came to worship because so many of their countrymen had had to leave Calumet to seek their fortunes elsewhere. St. Joseph's Church was reorganized in 1967 and a new parish was created. The old church was renamed St. Paul the Apostle. It serves all of the ethnic groups who in the past had their own national churches but whose children and grandchildren have moved away and become assimilated into American society. The Slovenians in Michigan depend on the Detroit area as the center of their current cultural activities. Slovenians migrated to Metro Detroit in the 1920s to find employment in the automobile and related industries. A large community flourished in Highland Park, a town surrounded by the city of Detroit. To serve their needs, St. John Vianney Church was opened in 1927. It continued as an active Slovenian parish until the early 1950s, when it was closed.

There have been very few Slovenian immigrants to the United States since the early 1950s, because the Republic of Slovenia's economic prosperity is equal to that of Austria. The country's inhabitants see no need to emigrate, as they did under Austro-Hungarian domination. There has been an increase of interest in their native language among Slovenian-American adults and children in the United States, but the numbers professing this interest still remain small. The descendants of the early pioneers have been American-born for some time now, and they will determine the connections with their cultural roots. The fact that Slovenia is now an independent country might play an important role in revivifying interest in Slovenian culture and language among all ages in the Slovenian community.

Macedonians

Macedonians are a South Slavic people who were citizens of the Republic of Macedonia, one of the constituent republics of the former Yugoslavia. In 1991 Macedonia declared its independence and it is known for the time being as the Former Yugoslav Republic of Macedonia (FYROM). The population of Macedonia is 2,200,000, of whom 67 percent are ethnic Slav Macedonians, with the largest minority being Albanian, who make up 21 percent of the population.[63] Outside of Macedonia, there are Macedonians in Greece and Bulgaria, as well as in other parts of the former Yugoslavia and Albania.

History of the Homeland

The ancient frontiers of Macedonia went beyond the present borders it shares with Serbia to the north, Bulgaria on the east, Albania on the west, and Greece to the south. During the Slavic migrations of the sixth and seventh centuries, when Macedonia was a part of the Byzantine Empire, it was settled by Slavs whom the Byzantine emperor Heraclius invited in 620 to establish themselves south of the Danube to serve as a buffer between Byzantium and the Avars. In the ninth century, much of northern Macedonia became part of the first Bulgarian Empire, which soon after divided in two. The western half, with its capital at Ohrid, became a state under Czar Samuel (997–1014), who made the archbishop of Ohrid the head of an independent church. Byzantium reconquered the kingdom in 1018 and held it for two centuries, until it regained its independence and became the Second Bulgarian Kingdom. In the middle of the fourteenth century, Serbia briefly ruled Macedonia, but the Ottoman Turks soon conquered most of the Balkans, with Macedonia falling under their sway from 1371 to 1912.

Although Bulgaria won its independence in 1878 at the Treaty of San Stefano, Macedonia remained under Turkish suzerainty, and even the Ilinden Uprising in 1903 failed to free it. Macedonia thereafter became prey to infiltrating groups of Bulgarians, Serbs, and Greeks, who fought each other and the Turks in an attempt to seize Macedonia for their respective countries. Leaders from within Macedonia forged the Internal Macedonian Revolutionary Organization (IMRO) with the goal of creating an independent state. After the Balkan wars of 1912–13 and World War I, Greece, Serbia, and Bulgaria partitioned Macedonia.

Even though Macedonian Slavs saw themselves as a separate Slavic people in the nineteenth century, their idea of a nation had been subsumed by a strong attachment to their individual villages (*selo*). It was not until after World War II that Macedonia came to be recognized as a republic of Yugoslavia. A Macedonian literary language began to develop, and in 1967 the Macedonian Orthodox Church became independent. Bulgaria and Greece, however, do not accept the existence of a distinct Macedonian nationality. With the secession of Macedonia from Yugoslavia in 1991, tensions with both countries have sharply increased.

Causes of Immigration and Settlement

After the 1903 Ilinden Uprising and the Turkish army's rampages against civilians, perhaps fifty thousand Macedonians escaped to the United States.[64] The early immigrants were for the most part single men from the areas around the western Macedonian towns of Kastoria, Florina, and Bitola. As often happened, they were generally recorded as emigrating from Turkey, Serbia, Bulgaria, or Greece. The majority were of

Macedonia

BIOGRAPHY

Michael Ilitch, who is from Bitola, Macedonia, is a very successful businessman in Detroit. He spent four years in the United States Marine Corps before opening a pizzaria. In 1959 he started Little Caesars restaurant, a franchise that he still owns. He received the Business Statesman award from the Harvard Business School Club of Detroit in 1990. He was given a Lester Patrick trophy for outstanding contributions to American hockey in 1991 and was the recipient of the Joe Louis award from *Sports Illustrated* magazine. He has also received citations from both the Reagan and Bush administrations. Since 1985 he has been the owner of Olympia Arenas, Inc. He founded Blue Line Distributing and Am's Pizza Café. He is the owner and president of the Detroit Red Wings hockey team, and has been the owner and chairman (and is a former president) of the Detroit Tigers baseball team and the Tigers' farm system for several years. He has also been recognized for his work for the National Trust for Historical Preservation.

ADDRESSES

- Macedonian Patriotic Organization and *Makedonska Tribuna* (Macedonian tribune), 124 West Wayne, Fort Wayne, IN 46802; (219) 422-5900, fax (219) 422-1348; *mtfw@macedonian.org*.

- St. Nativity of the Virgin Mary Church and Macedonian Folklore Group "Tanec," 21740 Ryan Street, Warren, MI 48093; (313) 757-3490.

- St. Clement Ohridski Bulgarian Eastern Orthodox Church, 19600 Ford Road, Dearborn, MI 48128; (313) 271-3110.

- Ilinden (Publisher of Macedonian and Serbo-Croatian works) and *Makendonski Zbor* (published monthly), 32344 Cambridge Street, Fraser, MI 48026; (313) 294-3974.

- Macedonian Ethnic Library, 920 Shorehem, Grosse Pointe Woods, MI 48236; (313) 886-3361.

- Macedonian Cultural Club SAR, 13518 Yvonne Street, Warren, MI 48089; (313) 839-3777.

peasant origin, and the others were skilled or semiskilled workers who socialized in cafes and boardinghouses. Present estimates suggest that there are probably thirty-five thousand Macedonians in Michigan.[65]

The Macedonian immigrants to Michigan sent money back home to help their families and relatives. They soon established grocery stores, restaurants, and bakeries in their new homeland; the majority of these enterprises in the Detroit area continue to be owned by Macedonian families. Most "Polish bakeries" in the Polish enclave of Hamtramck are actually operated by Macedonians.[66] These immigrants adopted Greek ethnicity when they opened restaurants or bakeries in order to simplify their complicated immigration history.

Macedonians living in the town of Bouf had to leave after World War I when Greece confiscated their fertile and prosperous tobacco lands. They had no choice but to emigrate, and most joined up with relatives from the 1903 wave of immigration to the United States.[67] These immigrants soon flocked to Dearborn, Dearborn Heights, and Detroit because of the lure of the burgeoning automobile industry and the good wages and eight-hour days provided by Henry Ford. They were also employed in other semiskilled jobs, such as construction, trucking, and the service industry. The story of Sam Brayant, who created the first Coney Island hot dog in Flint in 1919, typifies the entrepreneurial skills of these immigrants. Numerous Macedonian immigrants also arrived in Detroit from Canada in order to circumvent the 1924 Immigration Act quota.[68]

In the third wave of emigration, the Macedonian Slavs were forced to leave Greece in the harsh aftermath of World War II. Those who had lived in the Serb-dominated Macedonia, which became part of the new Yugoslavia, had fought on the royalist Četnik side against Tito's Partisans and were sponsored by Serbs from Detroit's St. Lazarus Serbian Orthodox Cathedral Ravanica. The Macedonians were seen by these Serbs as ethnically different because of their language and cultural distinctions, and the American-born Serbians did not mingle with them extensively. After the Greek Civil War of 1946–49, seventy thousand Macedonian Slavs emigrated from northern Greece to Canada, Australia, and the United States, settling mainly in the Midwest, especially in Michigan.[69] Entire villages were abandoned,

Michael and Marian Ilitch, owners of the Detroit Red Wings hockey team, with the coveted Stanley Cup. The Ilitchs both immigrated from Macedonia. After becoming a successful businessman, Mr. Ilitch has helped to stimulate the redevelopment of Detroit. Courtesy Ilitch Holdings, Inc.

with the inhabitants choosing to emigrate. The postwar population of Macedonians in Metro Detroit rose to thirty thousand. These immigrants did not always claim to be Macedonian, opting at times to be Greek, Bulgarian, or Yugoslav, depending upon the political wind. With the formation of the Yugoslav Macedonian Republic in 1944, Macedonians who immigrated could claim a national identity with their own Macedonian churches and language schools.

From 1969 to 1975, after Yugoslavia opened its borders to emigration, a fourth wave of Macedonian immigrants came to the United States. This exodus was due to the fact that Macedonia was not experiencing the economic development that was occurring in the more industrialized republics of the Yugoslav federation. During that period, the six thousand who settled in Michigan were peasants and workers emigrating from the countryside who had come in under the Refugee Relief Act of 1953 and the new immigration laws of 1965. In the Detroit area, they came from three areas of the Balkans: the Vardar area of Yugoslavia's Macedonia, Bulgaria, and the town of Bouf in Greece.[70] With the collapse of Yugoslavia, however, Macedonia emerged, amid controversy and opposition from Greece and Bulgaria, as a nation in 1991.

The Macedonians who migrated to Detroit settled in Hamtramck, which is a thriving Polish community that has attracted many South Slav and Middle Eastern immigrants. Most of the new arrivals were poor and lived in very small houses in the area. They immediately moved into the local economy and combined their efforts. They began to purchase bakeries, which they still own, throughout metropolitan Detroit. They do not mind the difficult and time-consuming labor involved, since they see good bread as a commodity most people will buy. This was an enterprise that immigrant Italians used to dominate, but the younger generations have not continued the tradition. Thus the Macedonians saw an opportunity for advancement, baking not only Macedonian breads but also French and Italian varieties. They soon began to mark the Detroit bakery business with their own particular cultural language and mystique. They have also expanded into very successful family-style and medium-sized restaurants that are moderately priced and unfranchised. Since Macedonians live in large extended families, their houses have tended to become quite large, with numerous rooms to accommodate family members. Because of their business acumen, many Macedonians have become financially secure and have moved into affluent Detroit suburbs.

Organizations and Politics

In 1922 the Macedonian community in Fort Wayne, Indiana, established the Macedonian Patriotic Organization, whose purpose was to further the cause of independence for Macedonia by influencing European and American political leadership. It soon became apparent, however, that it was a Bulgarian front organization whose Bulgarian and Macedonian agents were bent on dominating the Macedonian liberation movement for the advancement of Bulgarian interests. This organization is still in existence. Because of the community's varied background, it was very confusing when the word "Macedonian" appeared in the name of an organization, so the community in Detroit formed clubs that were named after the few towns from which they had emigrated. Within these small clubs they could get to know the other members well and to trust them. The exclusive nature of these clubs ensured that their members could feel that they were not being used for an ulterior motive. The Bouf's Benevolent Society, started in 1929, is one such club; Tetovo's Benevolent Society is likewise composed of members solely from the Tetovo area. This type of organization was typical until recent years, when larger groups, such as the Macedonian Cultural Center Ilinden (founded in 1976), were formed.

Before World War II Detroit became the most common destination for Macedonian immigrants; it had a population of seven thousand Macedonian Americans.[71] With the onset of the war, the All Slavic Congress convened in Detroit on 25 and 26 April 1942, from which emerged the American Slav Congress. The Macedonian-American People's League belonged to the latter. Macedonian Americans participated in the Michigan Slav Congress in Detroit in 1943 and helped create the United Committee of South Slavic Americans. There was also the International Workers Order, a communist movement in which South Slavs participated. These organizations opposed the U.S. government's increasing suspicion of the Soviet Union, which sparked the ire of American conservatives, who viewed the leftist Macedonian American organizations as fellow-travelers of the Soviet Union. In 1948 the House Committee on Un-American Activities and the attorney general of the United States accused the American Slav Congress and its affiliates of being directed from Moscow. Until 1955, alleged leftists, some of whom were prominent South Slavs, were subjected to witch-hunts by Congress. Numerous Macedonians were progressive in politics, and they supported the U.S. war effort in World War II and joined the military. At the conclusion of the war, they backed the Soviet Union and Yugoslavia.[72] George Pirinsky (born George Zaikoff) was a

Bulgarian Macedonian who was a prominent leader in the U.S. Communist Party. Because of their politics, however, many Macedonians left the United States or were deported.

The immigrants who left Yugoslavia after the 1965 Refugee Relief Act organized the United Macedonians in 1967, a group that remains in existence today and urges all Macedonians from whatever country to join their ranks. Since Toronto, Canada, has the largest number of Macedonian residents outside of the motherland, the organization's headquarters is located there. Detroit, which now is home to the largest Macedonian community in the United States, is the site of a branch office.[73] In the 1990s there has been an influx of Macedonians to Michigan, due to the instability in the Balkans. The voice of the community is the *Macedonian Tribune*, which is printed in Fort Wayne, Indiana; it first began publication in Minneapolis in 1927.

Religious and Cultural Life

During the Ottoman occupation, the Macedonians were part of the self-ruling Eastern Orthodox political community (the Ottoman millet social system based on religious affiliation), under Greek bishops. In the eighteenth and nineteenth centuries, however, they allied themselves with the Bulgarians in order to resist Greek dominance. When the Bulgarian Orthodox Church established its independence in 1870, Macedonians came under its jurisdiction, with Ottoman approval. The Macedonian Slavs later aided the Bulgarians in their movement to free Bulgaria and Macedonia from Turkish control.

Since 90 percent of Macedonians are Eastern Orthodox, when they came to the United States they joined Bulgarian parishes that adhered either to the Patriarch in Sofia, Bulgaria, or to the Bulgarian diocese of the Orthodox Church in America. Those Macedonians who became members of Bulgarian, Serbian, or Greek Orthodox parishes and organizations have merged with those communities, subsuming their cultural identities to those of the larger groups. In the St. Lazarus Serbian Orthodox parish in Detroit, a retired Orthodox priest ministered to Macedonian parishioners, although he is not officially part of St. Lazarus. In 1967 the Macedonian Orthodox Church chose to be

Macedonians in the traditional costumes in Detroit, 1931 (Reuther Library, Wayne State University).

governed by its own synod, resuming its existence after two centuries of inactivity following its dissolution by the Ottomans. In 1974 the Macedonians in Detroit organized a church committee that opened St. Nativity of the Virgin Mary Macedonian Orthodox Church under the metropolitan and Holy Synod of Skopje, Yugoslavia, and other communities in the state followed suit.

The most important cultural expression of the Macedonians is the *večerinka*, evening party, where folk dancing and music enable the participants to take pride in the world-renowned folk dance traditions of Macedonia. The ancient Macedonian folk dances are usually danced on Sundays and holidays. Dancing and singing have traditionally celebrated the end of harvest, but Christmas, Easter, St. George's Day, and

St. John's Eve are also occasions for dancing, as well as fairs and church festivals. People often don national costumes when they dance.

Macedonian dances are the most ancient of all South Slav dances, and are some of the oldest in the world. They are patterned after the ancient Thracian circle dances, which are called *oro* in Macedonian, *kolo* in Serbo-Croatian, *horos* in Greek, and *hora* in Romanian. *Oro* is a Thracian word that connotes leaping around in a circle; these are ecstatic Dionysian dances. The Macedonian *oro* steps are fast but complex, and must be carefully executed, with deliberate steps. Slowly the dance speeds up and assumes a more rhythmic quality. The "Bridal *Oro*" is a Macedonian dance that goes back to the ritualized dance of Thracian priestesses that is shown in a bas-relief of a stele found on the Greek island of Samothrace.

Another very ancient Macedonian dance is the "Russalia," which is danced during the Christmas and New Year winter solstice and has prehistoric roots. The Greek historian Xenophon (ca. 430–355 B.C.) wrote about this dance in his *Anabasis*. "Russalia" was adopted by Macedonian Slavs from pagan rituals and was transformed into a dance that symbolized their conversion to Christianity. In the performance of the dance, from twenty to sixty men, bearing wooden swords, dance in pairs in a circle while following two leaders who carry axes. They are clothed all in white, with short white skirts, fur caps, and a decorative red scarf across their chests. Accompanied by drums and flutes, the dancers perform slow steps and brandish their swords in a rhythmic pattern. These movements evoke healing of the sick and good harvests. The "Russalia" was traditionally performed in the various villages for twelve days, beginning on the first day of Christmas. The dancers could not speak, cross themselves, or pray for the entire period, since they represented the ancient pagans. They visited the sick in each village and crossed their swords over them for good health. On the twelfth day they entered the church in their native village, where they were "converted" to Christianity, and a lamb was killed in celebration.

In western Macedonia the dances resemble those in Albania: measured steps that are danced only by men, with drum and wind accompaniment. One such dance is "*Teskoto*" (Difficult), which is a shepherd dance with high leaps to represent jumping from rock to rock to watch for predators or bandits. It dates from pre-Slavic times and illustrates the Macedonians' hard life of border wars and raids, protecting their sheep, the land, and the tribe. These dances reveal their lives: the "*Aramijska Igra*" (Bandit's Dance) depicts an ambush, while the "*Kaladžijska Igra*" (Tinsmith's Dance), replicates the biannual ritual by which the tinsmiths would polish the peasants' brass vessels by rubbing them with their feet and moistened sand. Another Albanian dance, the *Čamče,* is performed by both men and women. It is a dignified, serious dance that is slow and stately, like a sarabande.

There are also Macedonian dances that are accompanied by only drums, and some with no accompaniment at all. The latter are strange, and are interrupted at times with cries. Rhythm and beat are counted by the dance's steps, by shouting, or by the jingling of coins or the jewelry decorating the women's dresses. The only sound is the thud of feet in harmony, and every now and then men will jump up for dramatic effect.[74] These ancient dances are cultural expressions that help divided Macedonians have a greater sense of their unique identity and serve to unify them as they bridge the gap between the old and the new.

Bosnian Muslims

osnian Muslims inhabit the republic of Bosnia-Herzegovina, which declared its independence from Yugoslavia in 1992. They constitute 44 percent of the total population; Serbs make up 31 percent and Croats 17 percent.[75] The three groups are identical ethnically and speak the same language, which has a number of words of Turkish origin.

Since the end of the the 1992–95 war, Bosnia has been recognized as a single state that is partitioned between the Muslim-Croat Federation, occupying 51 percent of the country's area, and the Serbian Republic, which covers 49 percent. The population of the state is 2,600,000, as compared to 4,300,000 before the Bosnian war.

Origins

The area now known as Bosnia was settled by Croats and Serbs in the sixth and seventh centuries. The kingdom of Bosnia fell to the Ottoman Turks in 1463, and the duchy of Herzegovina fell in 1482. During the four hundred years of Turkish occupation, large numbers of Bosnians converted to Sunni Islam. Bosnia-Herzegovina came under Austrian administration beginning in 1878 and was annexed by Austria-Hungary in 1908. It became part of Serbia with the creation of the Kingdom of the

Serbs, Croats, and Slovenes in 1918. In 1946 it constituted one of the six republics of Yugoslavia. Since the independence of Bosnia-Herzegovina in 1992, Muslims now refer to themselves as *Bosanci* or *Bosnjaci* (Bosnians).[76]

Causes of Immigration and Settlement

Bosnian Muslim immigration to the United States started in 1900, occurring later than that of the Slovenes, Croats, or Serbs. They had to flee after participating in the political protests against Austrian rule in 1899. Most came from around the towns of Gačko and Trebinje in Herzegovina, an impoverished and barren western region where farms were not modernized due to the Bosnian Muslim landowners' innate conservatism, especially after 1886, a situation that was also the case in Bosnia; both cases were a result of Ottoman rule.[77] As with immigrants from the other South Slav communities, the few hundred early Herzegovinian immigrants were young, unmarried peasants who had no intention of remaining in the United States. They set up a few cafes that later became social centers for the men from specific areas of Herzegovina. These cafes evolved from the original *Karaethane* in Mostar, Herzegovina, which was the Muslim Reading and Benevolent Society and was a coffeehouse where men could read newspapers, frequent lectures, and give financial aid to students and artisans.[78]

In 1908, when Austria-Hungary annexed Bosnia, a few thousand Bosnians emigrated, perhaps illegally, as the provincial records in Sarajevo show that only a few hundred emigrated between 1905 and 1914. Another group emigrated after the land reform of 1919 when the new Kingdom of the Serbs, Croats, and Slovenes expropriated land from Muslim landowners.

After World War II, a fourth wave of Bosnian Muslims arrived in the United States. This group was composed of refugees, displaced persons, and exiles who chose to emigrate from urban or rural areas due to political necessity. They had either enrolled in or been compelled to join Croatian fascist organizations during the war, and then had to escape for their lives once the war had ended. A small number had been part of the Četniks, a Serbian monarchist fighting force. Following the pattern of the other South Slavic groups who emigrated to America after the war, they were from all areas and social classes. Fleeing to Western Europe first, they were generally much better educated than their compatriots who had emigrated at the turn of the century. By the time this wave of immigrants arrived in the United States, the majority of the earlier Bosnian immigrants had either died or migrated to the West, particularly Los Angeles. The World War II refugees, who were very different from the earlier immigrants, did not get along well with them. The new refugees arrived in the old neighborhoods of Detroit, and the original settlers from Bosnia took second place as the new arrivals garnered white-collar jobs and abandoned the small ethnic enclaves of the pioneers. Some of the new immigrants had been rich landowners whose estates had been expropriated by the communist government in the 1950s, and thus their politics in the United States were tinged with anticommunism.

A fifth wave of immigrants arrived after 1965, when Yugoslavia lifted its ban on emigration to relieve the pressures of unemployment. These emigrants sought to employ their skills in France, West Germany, and Sweden, where many more opportunities were available to them than in Yugoslavia. A number later left Western Europe to come to the United States. They migrated mainly from rural areas, or from the small western Bosnian town of Gračanica, the Montenegrin town of Bar, on the Adriatic coast, or Sarajevo. These post-1965 immigrants were not as well educated as the postwar refugees, but their sentiments were less anticommunist than those of the 1950s immigrants. Then, in the late 1960s and early 1970s, a large number of single men and families emigrated from the countryside.[79]

The most recent arrivals from Bosnia have been refugees after the 1992–95 war began in Bosnia-Herzegovina. Two million refugees were forced to flee their homes for various destinations throughout the world during the war. The largest number of refugees in the United States have settled in Chicago, and there are sizeable communities in Milwaukee, Wisconsin, and Gary, Indiana. In Michigan, the Polish neighborhood of Hamtramck in Detroit is second to Chicago in the number of Bosnian refugees; Madison Heights and Dearborn also boast large Bosnian settlements. Seventy-five percent of Bosnian Muslims in the

Bosnia

MUSIC

The older Bosnian Muslims, and even the younger generation who have arrived in the United States since the Bosnian war started, still cling to traditional music. Its mainstay is the secular romantic ballad called the *sevdalinka* (from the Turkish word *sevdah*, which means "passion"), sung along with accordions, violin, and bass guitar. These melancholic tunes evoke intimacy and reflection; they are the Bosnian's connection with his or her motherland and Muslim culture. Turkish modes have influenced both religious music and the romantic ballad.

CUISINE

Bosnian cuisine has been influenced by Central Europe, the Balkans, and the Middle East. There are numerous meat dishes of lamb, pork, and beef. Two popular beef dishes are *ćevapčići* (sausage-shaped ground beef mixed with spices) and a hamburger patty (*pljeskavica*) grilled with onions that is put in a hefty pita bread. *Bosanski lonac* is a slow-roasted stew composed of layers of meat and vegetables served in a ceramic pot and eaten with whole-wheat bread. Dolmas, shish kabobs, salads, and baklava are other typical Bosnian offerings. Vegetables such as peppers, potatoes, or onions are stuffed with ground meat, rice, and other vegetables. Dolmas can be made from cabbage or grape leaves, kale, or any leafy vegetable that is large, then softened by cooking in order to surround a meat filling. The dolmas are placed in an amphora-shaped tureen, covered, and then slowly cooked over a low, covered fire. Pita can be filled with vegetables or meat, and pita meat pie is a meal in itself. *Burek* are great coils of crisp brown philo pastry filled with melted butter and tangy feta cheese, fried pumpkin, spiced apple, or the delicious *zeljanica*—a tasty mélange of cheese and spinach that is paradise on earth. *Slivovitz* (plum brandy) and *loza* (grape brandy) are popular alcoholic drinks, while Turkish coffee, *kefir* (a yogurt drink), and *salep* (a tea) are nonalcoholic favorites.

BOSNIAN MUSLIM RELIGIOUS CALENDAR

- *Five Daily Prayers:* They are called *sabah* (morning), *podnje* (noon), *ikindija* (afternoon), *aksam* (evening), and *jacija* (night).
- *Džuma:* Friday prayers at a mosque.

- *Hasure:* A celebration of the martyrdom of the Imam Hussein, the grandson of the prophet Muhammad. It falls on the tenth of Maharem, the first month of the Islamic calendar.

- *Ramazan (Ramadan):* The ninth month of the year during which the Qur'an began to be revealed to Muhammad. Muslims must fast from food and drink and abstain from sexual intercourse from dawn to dusk. It commences with the sighting of the waxing moon and concludes with its first appearance in the following month. Since it is calculated by the lunar calendar, it may occur in any season.

- *Ramazanski bajram:* A holiday inaugurated by a special prayer in the early morning of the day following the end of Ramazan. It consists of a three-day period of feasting and visiting other households.

- *Hadž:* The pilgrimage to Mecca that takes place two months after Ramazan.

- *Kurbanski bajram:* This festival marks the end of the pilgrimage season during which both pilgrims and those who stay home commemorate Abraham's willingness to sacrifice his son to Allah. It occurs two months and ten days after Ramazan, during the month of Zulhijje, and involves the killing of a sheep that is then roasted and distributed to the poor, and to relatives and friends. It is also called Hadžijski bajram in Bosnia-Herzegovina.

- *Mevlud:* A recital of a poem or poems in honor of the prophet Muhammad's birth. These recitals are held not on his birthday but on various days in the Islamic or Gregorian calendars. They are sometimes held in a mosque on the twelfth of the month of Rebiul Evvela (the anniversary of Muhammad's birth). A mevlud held in a home could celebrate the birth of a new family member, a marriage, moving into a new house, or any joyous event.

- *Dženaza:* A burial ceremony at which the prayers (*tevhid*) for the soul of the dead are recited. The corpse is wrapped in a white shroud, placed in a coffin without a lid, and covered with a green cloth.

BOSNIA-HERZEGOVINA INDEPENDENCE DAY

March 1.

ADDRESSES

- Bosnian-American Cultural Association, 1810 N. Pfingstan Road, North-brook, IL 60062; (312) 334-2323.
- Bosnian-American Islamic Center, Ramiz Aljovic, 3101 Roosevelt, Ham-tramck, MI 48212-3745.
- Friends of Bosnia, 85 Worcester Street, Suite 1, Boston, MA 02118; (617) 424-6752; *fob@crocker.com*; *http://www.crocker.com/~fob/*.

United States live in those six cities. Though the Bosnian war ended in 1995, as of 1999 there were more than fifty-five thousand Bosnian refugees living in the United States.

Organizations and Social Life

The Bosnian Muslims who settled in Detroit in the early part of this century used the coffeehouses as their social center. Many came from impoverished Herzegovina, finding unskilled jobs when they arrived. Their lodge, *Džemijetul Hajrije* (Benevolent Society), began in 1906 and functioned as a social and aid society and as a provider of medical insurance. Many of those pioneering immigrants remained bachelors, but some married other Slavs.

After World War II, Bosnian displaced persons began arriving in the United States. In an effort to care for them, a new organization was created in 1955—the Moslem Religious and Cultural Home (later changed to the Bosnian American Cultural Association). By the end of the 1950s, it published the *Glasnik Muslimana* (Muslim herald), which lasted only into the early 1960s.

In the small Bosnian Muslim community in Detroit, the better educated post–World War II immigrants became white-collar workers. Since 1965 the less-well-educated immigrants have tended to find work as skilled or semiskilled workers, machinists or carpenters, congregating in working-class areas.[80] Some have even ventured into business for themselves and done quite well. The World War II refugees identified themselves as Muslim Croats, and a small group called themselves Muslim Serbs. Since that time, however, they have come to see themselves as a separate national group, as recognized by the Tito government in 1971.

For Bosnian Muslims, religious belief has not been a strong component of their cultural affiliation. This is a personal decision, and there is no dogmatic aspect to it. In the United States, however, a number of immigrants, especially those who fled the Bosnian war, have experienced a close bond with Muslims from throughout the world as they have worshiped together in shared mosques.

Personal Histories

In the early 1970s Nino Crnovršanin, a bitter critic of the Tito government, fled Yugoslavia and settled in Detroit. He tried unsuccessfully to bring over Haris Zečević, a family friend living in Sarajevo, to study engineering before the Bosnian war started. By mid-1993, around two hundred Bosnian Muslims had arrived in Detroit, fleeing the war. In July 1993 Haris Zečević ended up in Detroit through the auspices of the U.S. Refugee Resettlement Office. His story reflects the tragic history of the Bosnian Muslims in the last decade of the twentieth century. His brother was killed while defending Sarajevo from the Bosnian Serb army. About two weeks after Haris's arrival, his mother was shot at the besieged Sarajevo airport while trying to join her son. She later died of her wounds. Haris got a job for a time at Nino Crnovršanin's metal-processing shop, where Ford components are fabricated. By 1994 there were over 1,000 Bosnian Muslims living in Detroit, and in 1996 alone 6,499 immigrated to the United States. Nino Crnovršanin has tried to help the Bosnian Muslims who have come to Detroit, and he has also worked hard to raise money for a Muslim Bosnia.[81]

Haris and most of the other Bosnian Muslims in the Detroit area live in the Polish enclave of Hamtramck. They have been trying to revive their uprooted culture in the vastness of their new city. They even have their own radio station that counters the Bosnian Serb radio broadcasts emanating from across the Detroit River in Windsor, Canada. Vildana, Haris's Sarajevo girlfriend, arrived in 1994, and they got married. The

South Slavs in Flint

On the east side of Flint was the St. John's Street district. Beginning in 1909 South Slavs began to settle the area. One of the earliest to arrive was Michael Pejakovich, a Croatian who operated a grocery store. Croatians ran hardware stores, groceries, and bars, and attended the local Catholic church. Another pioneer was a Macedonian, Žarko Nickoloff, who started the Balkan Bakery. Over the years many Macedonians owned and operated this and other bakeries in the community. Most of the Macedonians were from Tetovo, Yugoslavia, and maintained close relations with the neighboring Bulgarians. There were also a few Slovenians and Serbians in the neighborhood. Most of the men were employed in factories, the Buick plant, and the Fisher Body plant. Some of the women found jobs as sales clerks, waitresses, stenographers, machine operators, and teachers. The social life of the South Slav community centered around the Bulgarian-Macedonian Hall and the Croatian-Slovene Hall. Monthly dances (*večerinke*) were held, with music furnished by Detroit ethnic orchestras that traveled to Flint for the occasion.

St. Nicholas Russian Orthodox Church began to serve the Orthodox Slavs of the St. John's Street district in 1916. During the Depression they donated funds that saved the church. In 1944 the church was moved and dropped the term "Russian" in its name. During World War II, Slavic groups in the St. John's Street area formed a relief organization, the United American Slav Committee. Through picnics, dances, and shows they raised considerable sums of money that were sent abroad to relieve Slavic peoples that Hitler planned to destroy.

following year they had a son, Muris, named after his dead brother.[82] In 2002 Haris celebrated his thirty-third birthday in his adopted country; his son was seven years old. Vildana still prepares the Bosnian dishes: the meat and cheese pies, the rich, honeyed desserts of the East; and the roast lamb on spits. Yet they have also started on the age-old path of immigrants to a new land: those who have been uprooted have begun to set down roots.

Conclusion

South Slav immigrants have played an important if unsung role in American immigration history. American society has been transformed by the vast movement of immigrants from southern and eastern Europe, and the South Slavs have figured prominently in that transformation by forcing America, despite its reluctance, to open itself to all peoples. The process of South Slav migration, settlement, and assimilation into American society has been arduous and frustrating, taking its toll on many immigrants. A number have suffered discrimination and persecution for their way of life and political beliefs, some even losing their rights to remain in this country. The scars of that traumatic migration of South Slavs, as of all those who have transplanted themselves into a new country, have continued to mark later generations. Oscar Handlin has written in *The Uprooted* that "the history of immigration is a history of alienation and its consequences."[83] The hardships of the South Slavs ought to serve as a cautionary tale to all Americans, especially in these uncertain times.

South Slav Recipes

What people eat as food represents a cultural expression as much as artistic production. Here are a few South Slav recipes that illustrate that fact.

Sarma/Stuffed Cabbage *(Danica Radonich)*

2 small cabbages, cored	1½ lbs. pork
½ cup of vinegar	salt and pepper to taste
4–5 onions	½ cup of rice
4 garlic cloves	1 can tomato soup
½ lb. bacon	1 can tomato sauce
2 lbs. ground beef	1 large can sauerkraut

Boil cored cabbages in water and vinegar until the leaves fall off; separate individual leaves. Trim middle vein on each leaf (cut out or make thin as the leaf). In a pan, sauté onions, garlic, and bacon. Add beef, pork, salt, and pepper, and mix well. Parboil rice, and add to meat mixture. Roll meat mixture into cabbage leaves and place in pan. Mix tomato soup, tomato sauce, one can of water, and sauerkraut. Pour tomato mixture over cabbage rolls. Bake at 350° for one hour. *Serves 8.*

Kupus i Grah/Cabbage and Beans *(Millie Goich)*

small bag pinto beans
2 smoked ham hocks
2 medium onions, diced
1 Tbsp. vegetable oil

8 Tbsp. flour
1 can tomato soup
1 can of hock broth
1 large can sauerkraut (drained and rinsed)

Soak beans overnight in water. Drain soaking water. Add fresh water to cover beans and ham hocks. Cook together for 1½–2 hours.

Then, in a separate pan sauté diced onions in oil; add flour, and brown (roux), and stir over low heat. Add tomato soup and hock broth, and cook for 10 minutes. Add sauerkraut and tomato mixture to the beans. Cook for another 20 minutes. *Serves 6.*

Srbska Salata/Serbian Salad *(traditional)*

1 large onion, cut into rings, then halved
1 large green pepper, cut into 1½-inch pieces
2 large tomatoes, cut into eighths
½ cup white vinegar
2 Tbsp. vegetable oil
1 Tbsp. snipped parsley

1 clove garlic, crushed
½ tsp. salt
⅛ tsp. pepper

Place onion, green pepper, and tomato into glass bowl. Shake vinegar, oil, parsley, garlic, salt, and pepper in a tightly covered jar. Pour dressing over vegetables; stir until coated. Cover and refrigerate at least 3 hours and no longer than 24 hours. *Serves 4.*

Kolačvi s Pekmezom/Jam Squares *(Stella Todorov)*

¾ lb. butter
1 cup sugar
grated peel of 1 lemon
1 tsp. cinnamon
1 tsp. cloves

3 egg yolks
½ cup milk
3 cups flour, sifted
1 tsp. baking powder
jam

Cream butter. Add sugar and cream again. Add grated lemon peel, cinnamon, cloves, yolks, milk, flour, and baking powder. Blend well until you have a soft dough. Set aside ¼ of the dough and roll out the rest on a floured board to fit a shallow, square, greased pan. Place dough in pan and spread with any desired jam. Roll out the rest of the dough. Lattice strips over the top and bake in a 350° oven until lightly browned—about 30 minutes.

Kifle *(Sophie Dukich)*

2 sticks butter
2 cups sifted flour
8 oz. cream cheese

apricot jam
powdered sugar

At room temperature mix butter and cream cheese in bowl. Mix in sifted flour; divide the dough into 4 balls. Chill 3 hours or overnight. Roll each ball between wax paper to the size of approximately 10" × 15". Keep the dough chilled. Cut into 2½" squares. Fill with approximately ½ teaspoon of apricot jam, fold two sides kitty-corner to the center and press. Bake 350° until lightly brown. Cool and dust with powdered sugar. *Makes 50 cookies.*

Kafa Balkanska/Balkan Coffee *(traditional)*

1 demitasse cup boiling water
1 heaping tsp. extra fine ground coffee
1 tsp. sugar

Place water in brass coffee maker. Add sugar and coffee and stir vigorously. Place over heat and bring to a boil. Remove from heat until foam goes down, then replace over heat. Repeat this 3 times to insure good coffee. Pour into demitasse cup, holding coffee maker high over cup and then bringing it down toward cup so a light foam forms. Do not add cream or stir.

Notes

1. Richard Hofstadter, William Miller, and Daniel Aaron, *The United States: The History of a Republic* (Englewood Cliffs, N.J.: Prentice Hall, 1967), 693.
2. Francis H. Eterovich and Christopher Spalatin, eds., *Croatia: Land, People, Culture* (Toronto: University of Toronto Press, 1970), 1:81–83.
3. The first Croatian immigrants to the United States were Dalmatians who arrived in the seventeenth and eighteenth centuries.
4. John Bodnar, *The Transplanted: A History of Immigrants in Urban America* (Bloomington: Indiana University Press, 1985), 12.
5. Gerald G. Govorchin, *Americans from Yugoslavia* (Gainesville: University of Florida Press, 1961), 8–19.
6. Louis Adamic, *From Many Lands* (New York: Harper and Brothers, 1940), 55–67.
7. Anthony Lucas spelled his last name with a *c* instead of a *k*. Ivan Čizmić, *Hrvati u Životu Sjedinjenih Američkih Država* (Zagreb: Biblioteka Globus, 1982), 98.
8. Stephan Thernstrom, Ann Orlov, Oscar Handlin, eds., "Croats," in *Harvard Encyclopedia of American Ethnic Groups* (Cambridge: Belknap Press of Harvard University Press, 1980), 251.
9. Jerry Stanley, *Big Annie of Calumet: A True Story of the Industrial Revolution* (New York: Crown Publishers, 1996), 19.

10. Emily G. Balch, *Our Slavic Fellow Citizens* (New York: Charities Publication Committee, 1910), 176.

11. Stanley, *Big Annie*, 46.

12. George Prpic, *The Croatian Immigrants in America* (New York: Philosophical Library, 1971), 157–58.

13. Anthony Lucas later supported the first miners' compensation law in the state, and went on to become the first Croatian elected to the Michigan legislature.

14. Clarence A. Andrews, "Big Annie and the 1913 Michigan Copper Strike," *Michigan History*, 57, no. 1 (spring 1973): 57–68.

15. Govorchin, *Americans from Yugoslavia*, 77–78.

16. Čizmić, *Hrvati u Životu*, 90–93.

17. Ibid., 92, 93, 208.

18. Bodnar, *The Transplanted*, 2.

19. Mark Wyman, *Round-Trip to America: The Immigrants Return to Europe, 1880–1930* (Ithaca, N.Y.: Cornell University Press, 1993), 10.

20. Hofstadter, Miller, and Aaron, *The United States*, 694.

21. Daniel Cetinich, "Croatians," in *American Immigrant Cultures: Builders of a Nation*, ed. David Levinson and Melvin Ember (New York: Macmillan Reference USA, 1997), 1:193.

22. Čizmić, *Hrvati u Životu*, 238.

23. Bodnar, *The Transplanted*, 13, 14.

24. John Bodnar, "Materialism and Morality: Slavic-American Immigrants and Education, 1890–1940," *Journal of Ethnic Studies* 3, no. 4 (winter 1976): 7.

25. Čizmić, *Hrvati u Životu*, 94.

26. Edward Ifkovic, "Croatian Americans," in *Gale Encyclopedia of Multicultural America*, 2d ed., ed. Jeffrey Lehman (Farmington Hills, Mich.: Gale Group, 2000), 2:380.

27. Antoine Ivan Rezek, *History of the Diocese of Sault Ste. Marie and Marquette* (Chicago: M. A. Donohue & Co., 1906–7): 2:286.

28. Ružica and Alojzije Kapetanović, *Croatian Cuisine* (Scottsdale, Ariz.: Associated Book Publishers, 1992).

29. A. A. Vasiliev, *History of the Byzantine Empire* (Madison: University of Wisconsin Press, 1961), 2:17–21.

30. Harold W. V. Temperley, *History of Serbia*, (1917; reprint, New York: AMS Press, 1970), 100–105.

31. Michael B. Petrovich and Joel Halpern, "Serbs," in *Harvard Encyclopedia of American Ethnic Groups,* ed. Stephan Thernstrom, Ann Orlov, Oscar Handlin (Cambridge: Belknap Press of Harvard University Press, 1980), 918. Prior to 1912, twenty thousand Montenegrins had emigrated to the United States. This was one-tenth of Montenegro's population at the time, and a greater percentage of its males.

32. Jerome Kisslinger, *The Serbian Americans* (New York and Philadelphia: Chelsea House Publishers, 1990), 41–42.

33. Ibid., 26.

34. Joel M. Halpern and Barbara Kerewsky Halpern, *A Serbian Village in Historic Perspective* (New York: Holt, Rinehart, and Winston, 1972), 40–41.

35. Kisslinger, 44–45.

36. Ibid., 44.

37. In the Balkan Wars, Serbia, Bulgaria, Greece, and Montenegro fought against Turkey. The Bulgarians later also attacked Greece and Serbia.

38. Bodnar, *The Transplanted,* 18–23.

39. [Karen Todorov], "Serbians," in *Ethnic Groups in Michigan,* ed. James M. Anderson and Iva A. Smith, in The Peoples of Michigan Series (Detroit: Ethnos Press, 1983), 246.

40. Čizmić, *Hrvati u Životu,* 142.

41. John Milich, "She Stands Alone," *Serb World USA* 3, no. 6 (July/August 1987): 401.

42. June Miljevich Raynal, "Living and Logging: The Miljevich Story," *Serb World USA,* 4, no. 5 (May/June 1988): 41.

43. This information was submitted by Paulina Mijatovich in a letter dated 30 June 1993.

44. Roger Cohen, *Hearts Grown Brutal: Sagas of Sarajevo* (New York: Random House, 1998), 283–84.

45. Paulina Mijatovich, *Seventy-Fifth Anniversary of the Parish of St. Lazarus Serbian Orthodox Cathedral Ravanica* (Detroit: Ravanica Press, 1990), 2, 3, 5, 9.

46. Ibid., 4.

47. Daniel Obed, "Slovenes," in *Ethnic Groups in Michigan, The Peoples of Michigan Series,* ed. James M. Anderson and Iva A. Smith (Detroit: Ethnos Press, 1983), 254.

48. Rudolph M. Susel, "Slovenes," in *Harvard Encyclopedia of American Ethnic*

Groups, ed. Stephan Thernstrom, Ann Orlov, Oscar Handlin (Cambridge: Belknap Press of Harvard University Press, 1980), 935.

49. Willis F. Dunbar, *Michigan: A History of the Wolverine State,* rev ed. by George S. May (Grand Rapids, Mich.: William B. Eerdmans Publishing Co., 1980), 297.

50. George Prpic, *South Slavic Immigration to America* (Boston: Twayne Publishers, 1978), 146.

51. Marie Prisland, *From Slovenia—To America: Recollection and Collections* (Chicago: Slovenian Woman's Union of America, 1968), 90–91, 111.

52. June N. Miljevic, "The Yugoslav People in Michigan," *Michigan History* 25, no. 3 (summer/autumn 1941): 358.

53. Prisland, *From Slovenia,* 114.

54. Barbara McCann, "Women of Traunik: A Story of Slovenian Immigration," *Michigan History* 68, no. 1 (January/February 1984): 42.

55. Ivan (John) Molek, *Slovene Immigrant History, 1900–1950: Autobiographical Sketches,* trans. Mary Molek (Dover, Del.: M. Molek, 1979), 55, 85, 100–101, 154.

56. Russell M. Magnaghi, "Eastern Europeans in Marquette County," *Harlow's Wooden Man* 21, no. 2 (spring 1985): 9.

57. Prisland, *From Slovenia,* 115.

58. Čizmić, *Hrvati u Životu,* 14243.

59. Obed, "Slovenes," 254.

60. Prisland, *From Slovenia,* 112.

61. Bodnar, Materialism and Morality, 10.

62. Ibid., 8.

63. Elizabeth Shostak, "Macedonian Americans," in *Gale Encyclopedia of Multicultural America,* 2d ed., ed. Jeffrey Lehman (Farmington Hills, Mich.: Gale Group, 2000), 2:1161.

64. Stephan Thermstrom, Ann Orlov, Oscar Handlin, eds. "Macedonians" in *Harvard Encyclopedia of Ethnic Groups* (Cambridge: Belknap Press of Harvard University Press, 1980), 691.

65. Dusan Sinadinoski, "Macedonians," in *Ethnic Groups in Michigan,* ed. James M. Anderson and Iva A. Smith, The Peoples of Michigan Series (Detroit: Ethnos Press, 1983), 196.

66. Information obtained from an interview of Peter Slavcheff by Russell M. Magnaghi in 1993.

67. Ibid.

68. Shostak, "Macedonain Americans," 2:1163.

69. Thernstrom, Orlov, Handlin, "Macedonians," 691.

70. Sinadinoski, "Macedonians," 196.

71. Peter Vasiliadis, "Macedonians," in *American Immigrant Cultures: Builders of a Nation,* ed. David Levinson and Melvin Ember (New York: Macmillan, 1997), 2:598.

72. Shostak, "Macedonian Americans," 2:1169.

73. Ibid., 2:1164.

74. Stoyan Pribichevich, *Macedonia: Its People and History* (University Park, Penn.: Pennsylvania State University Press, 1982), 221–23.

75. Noel Malcolm, *Bosnia: A Short History* (New York: New York University Press, 1994), 223.

76. Daniel Cetinich, "Bosnian Muslims," in *American Immigrant Cultures: Builders of a Nation,* ed. David Levinson and Melvin Ember (New York: Macmillan Reference USA, 1997), 1:95.

77. Bodnar, *The Transplanted,* 26.

78. Robert Donia, *Islam under the Double Eagle* (Boulder, Colo.: Eastern European Monographs, 1981), 177.

79. Cetinich, "Bosnian Muslims," 1:96.

80. Ibid., 1:97.

81. Cohen, *Hearts Grown Brutal,* 228–29, 281–82, 320.

82. Ibid., 324–25.

83. Oscan Handlin, *The Uprooted: The Epic Story of the Great Migrations That Made the American People* (Boston: Little, Brown, 1951), 4.

For Further Reference

Adamic, Louis. *From Many Lands*. New York: Harper and Brothers, 1940.

Andrews, Clarence A. "'Big Annie' and the1913 Michigan Copper Strike." *Michigan History* 57, no. 1 (spring 1973): 53–68.

Balch, Emily G. *Our Slavic Fellow Citizens*. New York: Charities Publication Committee, 1910.

Bodnar, John. "Materialism and Morality: Slavic-American Immigrants and Education, 1890–1940." *Journal of Ethnic Studies* 3, no. 4 (winter 1976): 1–19.

———. *The Transplanted: A History of Immigrants in Urban America*. Bloomington: Indiana University Press, 1985.

Cetinich, Daniel. "Bosnian Muslims." In *American Immigrant Cultures: Builders of a Nation*, edited by David Levinson and Melvin Ember, 1:95–99. New York: Macmillan Reference USA, 1997.

———. "Croatians." In *American Immigrant Cultures: Builders of a Nation*, edited by David Levinson and Melvin Ember, 1: 191–95. New York: Macmillan Reference USA, 1997.

Čizmić, Ivan. *Hrvati u Životu Sjedinjenih Američkih Država*. Zagreb: Biblioteka Globus, 1982.

Cohen, Roger. *Hearts Grown Brutal: Sagas of Sarajevo*. New York: Random House, 1998.

"Croats." In *Harvard Encyclopedia of American Ethnic Groups*, 247–56. Cambridge: Belknap Press of Harvard University Press, 1980.

Donia, Robert. *Islam under the Double Eagle*. Boulder, Colo.: Eastern European Monographs, 1981.

Dunbar, Willis F. *Michigan: A History of the Wolverine State*. Rev. ed. By George S. May. Grand Rapids, Mich.: William B. Eerdmans Publishing Co., 1980.

Eterovich, Francis H., and Christopher Spalatin, eds. *Croatia: Land, People, Culture*. 2 vols. Toronto: University of Toronto Press, 1970.

Govorchin, Gerald G. *Americans from Yugoslavia*. Gainesville: University of Florida Press, 1961.

Halpern, Joel M., and Barbara Kerewsky Halpern. *A Serbian Village in Historic Perspective*. New York: Holt, Rinehart and Winston, 1972.

Handlin, Oscar. *The Uprooted: The Epic Story of the Great Migrations That Made the American People*. Boston: Little, Brown, 1951.

Hofstadter, Richard, William Miller, and Daniel Aaron. *The United States: The History of a Republic*. Englewood Cliffs, N.J.: Prentice Hall, 1967.

Ifkovic, Edward. "Croatian Americans." In *Gale Encyclopedia of Multicultural America*, edited by Jeffrey Lehman, 2d ed., 1:460–72. Farmington Hills, Mich.: Gale Group, 2000.

Kapetanović, Ružica, and Alojzije Kapetanović. *Croatian Cuisine*. Scottsdale, Ariz.: Associated Book Publishers, 1992.

Kisslinger, Jerome. *The Serbian Americans*. New York and Philadelphia: Chelsea House Publishers, 1990.

Lockwood, William G. "Bosnian Muslims." In *Harvard Encyclopedia of American Ethnic Groups*, edited by Stephan Thernstrom, Ann Orlov, Oscar Handlin, 184–86. Cambridge: Belknap Press of Harvard University Press, 1980.

Magnaghi, Russell M. "Eastern Europeans in Marquette County." *Harlow's Wooden Man* 21, no. 2 (spring 1985): 9–11.

Malcolm, Noel. *Bosnia: A Short History*. New York: New York University Press, 1994.

McCann, Barbara. "Women of Traunik: A Story of Slovenian Immigration." *Michigan History* 68, no. 1 (January/February 1984): 41–45.

Mijatovich, Paulina, St. Clair Shores, Mich., to Russell M. Magnaghi, Marquette, Mich., 30 June 1993. Russell M. Magnaghi Collection, Northern Michigan University, Marquette, Michigan.

————. *Seventy-Fifth Anniversary of the Parish of St. Lazarus Serbian Orthodox Cathedral Ravanica*. Detroit: Ravanica Press, 1990.

Milich, John. "She Stands Alone." *Serb World USA* 3, no. 6 (July/August 1987): 40–43.

Miljevic, June N. "The Yugoslav People in Michigan." *Michigan History* 25, no. 3 (summer/autumn 1941): 358–64.

Molek, Ivan (John). *Slovene Immigrant History, 1900–1950: Autobiographical Sketches*. Translated by Mary Molek. Dover, Del.: M. Molek, 1979.

Obed, Daniel. "Slovenes." In *Ethnic Groups in Michigan, The Peoples of Michigan Series*, edited by James M. Anderson and Iva A. Smith, 252–55. Detroit: Ethnos Press, 1983.

Petrovich, Michael B., and Joel Halpern. "Serbs." In *Harvard Encyclopedia of American Ethnic Groups*, edited by Stephan Thernstrom, Ann Orlov, Oscar Handlin, 916–26. Cambridge: Belknap Press of Harvard University Press, 1980.

Pribichevich, Stoyan. *Macedonia: Its People and History*. University Park: Pennsylvania State University Press, 1982.

Prisland, Marie. *From Slovenia—To America: Recollection and Collections*. Chicago: Slovenian Woman's Union of America, 1968.

Prpic, George. *The Croatian Immigrants in America*. New York: Philosophical Library, 1971.

————. *South Slavic Immigration to America*. Boston: Twayne Publishers, 1978.

Raynal, June Miljevich. "Living and Logging: The Miljevich Story." *Serb World USA* 4, no. 5 (May/June 1988): 40–43.

Rezek, Antoine Ivan. *History of the Diocese of Sault Ste. Marie and Marquette*. 2 vols. Chicago: M. A. Donohue & Co., 1906–7.

Shostak, Elizabeth. "Macedonian Americans." In *Gale Encyclopedia of Multicultural America*, edited by Jeffrey Lehman, 2d ed., 2:1161–72. Farmington Hills, Mich.: Gale Group, 2000.

Sinadinoski, Dusan. "Macedonians." In *Ethnic Groups in Michigan*. The Peoples of Michigan Series, edited by James M. Anderson and Iva A. Smith, 194–97. Detroit: Ethnos Press, 1983.

Slavcheff, Peter. Interview by Russell M. Magnaghi, 12 April 1993. Russell M. Magnaghi Collection, Northern Michigan University, Marquette, Michigan.

Stanley, Jerry. *Big Annie of Calumet: A True Story of the Industrial Revolution*. New York: Crown Publishers, 1996.

Susel, Rudolph M. "Slovenes." In *Harvard Encyclopedia of American Ethnic Groups,* edited by Stephan Thernstrom, Ann Orlov, Oscar Handlin, 934–42. Cambridge: Belknap Press of Harvard University Press, 1980.

Temperley, Harold W. V. *History of Serbia.* 1917. Reprint, New York: AMS Press, 1970.

[Todorov, Karen]. "Serbians." In *Ethnic Groups in Michigan.* The Peoples of Michigan Series, edited by James M. Anderson and Iva A. Smith, 244–48. Detroit: Ethnos Press, 1983.

Vasiliadis, Peter. "Macedonians." In *American Immigrant Cultures: Builders of a Nation,* edited by David Levinson and Melvin Ember, 2:597–602. New York: Macmillan Reference USA, 1997.

Vasiliev, A. A. *History of the Byzantine Empire.* 2 vols. Madison: University of Wisconsin Press, 1961.

Wyman, Mark. *Round-Trip to America: The Immigrants Return to Europe, 1880–1930.* Ithaca, N.Y.: Cornell University Press, 1993.

Index